NUMBER 24
JUNE 1978

Managing Editor Robert Gardiner
Editor John Bowen, CEng, MRINA
Art Editor Ray Fishwick
Consultant Editor Arthur L Tucker

model Shipwright

CONTENTS

© **1977 Conway Maritime Press Ltd.** All articles published in *Model Shipwright* are strictly copyright and may not be reproduced without the written consent of the publishers
ISBN 0 85177 123 8
Published quarterly by Conway Maritime Press Ltd., 2 Nelson Road, Greenwich, London SE10 9JB.
Telephone 01-858 7211
Subscription Rates in UK £7 post paid for four issues published in September, December, March and June. Other rates on application.

Typesetting by Format Print Ltd., Erith, Kent.
Printed and bound in the United Kingdom by Page Bros (Norwich) Ltd.

COMMENT

The growing and widening readership of *Model Shipwright* soon come to appreciate the value of the journal to modelmakers, and for those who have joined our ranks in recent years the big disappointment has been to find that the early issues are out of print. Indeed copies of the first few numbers have become something of collectors' items. To meet the requests from many subscribers, and to help those whose interest in the journal is of more recent origin, the publishers have decided to reprint a limited edition of the first four numbers as a single bound volume; this will be available later this year.

We have omitted the customary index from the current issue, since we hope to publish at a later date a cumulative index covering all 24 or more numbers of the journal; further information will be given in this column once the details have been finalised.

A view of the new Glasgow Museum model ship gallery. In the foreground is HMS *Howe* and on the right is HMS *Hood*. *Photo: Courtesy Glasgow Museum of Transport*

Plans Service We are pleased to announce that agreement has been reached with Maritime Models Ltd, 7 Nelson Road, Greenwich, London SE10 whereby this company will undertake the marketing of all the plans in the Model Shipwright Plan Service. With effect from the 1 June 1978 these plans will be available exclusively from that organisation, and all orders should be sent to them at the above address. Readers will be kept informed, of course, through this journal of additions to the Service.

The importance of ship models has been emphasised in two very diverse ways in our post in recent weeks. Up in Scotland the Glasgow District Council has completed the new ship model hall and gallery in their Museum of Transport in Albert Drive, Glasgow, and it was officially opened by Prince Charles on the 23 February 1978. The Glasgow collection of ship models is among the largest and most representative in the world, and the authorities have long been handicapped through lack of space to do justice to this remarkable collection. Two years ago I stood in this large empty building — it was formerly part of a tram depot — and listened to Anthony Browning's plans to create therein a means of displaying at least a major part of the valuable collection of models under his care. The Clyde Room is the result — a gallery designed and laid out in accordance with the most modern concepts of visual display. Here can be seen models ranging in size from a few inches to the 17 ft long *Queen Mary*,

and including Clyde steamers, merchant ships, cross channel ships, passenger liners, yachts, warships, sailing ships, dredgers, and many other vessels. The Museum has a particularly good collection of prisoner-of-war bone models.

The Mariners Museum, Newport News, Virginia 23606, USA has announced its first International Model Ship Craftsman Competition. Full details and entry forms can be obtained from the Museum. Entry is free, and the deadline for the submission of completed models is the 1 June 1980. The competition is open to amateur and professional model builders, and there will be four categories: **1** Kit models; **2** modified kit models; **3** modified scratch-built models, that is, those in which some commercially fabricated parts have been used **4** wholly scratch-built models. In each class there will be sections for adults and juniors (under 18 years on 1-6-80). The aim of the competition is to encourage excellence of craftsmanship in model shipbuilding, and the criteria for judging will include uniformity and accurancy of scale, authenticity, neatness of finish, rigging, fittings, masting and hull. Following judging, selected entries will be exhibited at the Mariners Museum between 15 June and 1 September 1980.

From Australia we hear that moves are afoot to establish an organisation to be called the *Maritime History Society of Australia*. 'In the Society all interested individuals and institutions will be able to join forces to deepen and broaden their interests and together foster and further development of Maritime History in Australia'. These and the other aims and plans for the Society are laid out in detail in a most interesting brochure which can be obtained from Mr A C Staples, 66 Melville Parade, South Perth, Western Australia 6151. We are sure that all our readers will join in wishing the Steering Committee every success in their venture. The importance of research and the preservation of knowledge has long been a theme of ours, and Australia has much to offer the maritime historian. It is good to think that this valuable material will not be lost. **John Bowen**

US GUNBOAT NUMBER 12

by Clem Robinson

While still at school Clem Robinson built working models of square riggers which did well at a number of Model Engineer exhibitions. However, this gunboat is his first model since his schooldays, his career as a research engineer having kept him from his hobby for some time.

This vessel was built by Jacob Coffin at Newburyport, Massachusetts in 1805. The ancestry of *Number 12* can be traced back to the gunboats borrowed from the kingdom of Naples in 1804 when the Americans were engaged in operations against the Barbary regency of Tripoli. The gunboats were returned, but their design was taken back to America after the war. It showed, in effect, an enlarged ship's boat, decked, some 63 ft long with one mast lateen rigged, and a jib, carrying one large gun. This type of vessel was known as a 'parancelle'.

The 'Act Pertaining to the Navy', passed by the Seventh Congress on

28 February 1803, authorised the construction or purchase of four vessels of not more than 16 guns, and 15 gunboats — the Naval constructors were asked for their proposals. Captain Edward Preble proposed a series of designs. His third and fourth designs were basically similar; *Number 12* was built from the fourth design, which showed a somewhat larger vessel than number three. The vessel is still an enlarged ship's boat 66 ft long on deck, a beam of 18 ft with a square tuck transome stern. She draws 3 ft forward and 5 ft aft, and has bilge keels to improve the sailing qualities of such a shallow hull — as required for working close inshore and in rivers and shallow waters. Captain Preble's designs three and four show a simple schooner rig of quite low profile, a gaff main, a sliding gunter fore and one jib. This very simple rig is not at all in keeping with the usual American idea of clouds of canvas. It is likely that this particular rig was employed on only a few vessels, possibly only two, and the possibility that their rigs may have been altered in service cannot be ruled out.

Number 12's gun mounting is a very unusual one. Apparently Captain Preble made the acquaintance of an inventor named Hawkins who had worked on the problems of recoil when firing large guns of 18, 24 or 32 pounds calibre from small boats. If such a gun was fired on a bearing other than straight along the axis of the hull the recoil could at worst capsize the vessel, and at least would produce such a roll as to make it impossible to fire the gun again for some time. Hawkins' solution to the problem had a simplicity amounting almost to genius; he mounted two guns on a circular horizontal rotating platform, one each side, pointing in opposite directions. It seems that there was some sort of 'hinge' which permitted the gun to recoil some 4 inches to maintain the accuracy of aim, after which the recoil acted upon the wheel, rotating it. This 'hinge' was possibly a pin in a slot arrangement, but the obvious advantages of the mount are clear; its recoil is mostly taken up in the gun mount and not transmitted to the hull and there is a second gun and crew firing alternately which would

double the rate of fire of a one gun mounting. The gun mounting was built and tested and found quite practical by all concerned. It is an example of the American innovative spirit and it is odd that Hawkins' wheel should have been fitted to only three gunboats, *Numbers 11, 12* and *13,* out of the total of over a hundred.

Number 12, although built in Massachusetts, was employed on the New Orleans station and was broken up in 1812, by which time her odd gun mount had been removed. Gunboat *Number 11* was a sort of sister ship to *Number 12.* She was built about the same time as *Number 12* and to the same design, but by a different builder. While the resultant vessel was presumably very similar to *Number 12,* her dimensions differed in several respects. She was, for example, several feet longer so that the two vessels were by no means identical. Most of the American gunboats were designed to row as well as sail, in fact, they were often referred to as galley gunboats. These boats were fitted with long hatch structures on deck, which were rowing frames. They contained seats. It appears that they gave access to the hull below deck and would, therefore, have to be covered at sea or when not being used for rowing.

These American gunboats are interesting craft. For example, some designs were intended to sail in either direction. A splendid book by Howard I Chappelle called *The History of the American Sailing Navy* contains a wealth of information — too much for one lifetime's modelling. Perhaps one day I shall build another gunboat but I'm not sure yet where I shall send it.

Construction of the model embodies no great advances in technology. The hull is carved from solid and the decks are planked. There is, in my humble opinion, no substitute whatsoever for a deck made of planks. Working on a general rule of thumb means that there are two planks to a foot, although it is always best to check your prototype, if you can. Longridge on the *Cutty Sark* quoted five inches as the width of deck planks, while on the *Victory* it is my recollection that they are about nine inches. Be that as it may, the requirement is for wood whose thickness is

equal to the width of the plank in question. In the case of *Number 12* one sixteenth sheet hardwood (I used obeche) is made to order. Cut from the standard 3 ft x 3 in sheet pieces of wood as long as a plank. Again quoting Longridge, 20 ft seems to be an appropriate length. While you are about it, cut an odd length to give planks of 24 ft or 25 ft or even 30 ft, for which I will give a reason later. The treatment I use on these bits of sheet which you now have is to sand lightly and apply sanding sealer (or whatever) to lay the grain. When dry and sanded again paint the flat sides and the end grain ends black. I used Belco. By now it is fairly obvious that application of a straight ruler and razor blade will cut from the 'plank blanks' a series of planks (of a thickness which will probably vary wildly — but not to worry), which are already caulked along both sides and at the ends — useful that. The whole deck is scraped and rubbed down after laying so that the thickness of the cut planks is not important.

Study of a properly planked deck reveals that there are mitred surrounds to the masts and to the major deck openings and fittings. A prepared piece of sheet to give planking of say nine or twelve inch planks should have been mentioned earlier. These wider planks are used for the king plank down the vessel's centre line, and to make the mitred openings in the deck. Details of how to lay a deck with the butts correctly spaced are given in C N Longridge's works on the *Cutty Sark* and *Victory.*

At this point I should point out that while laying deck planks 1/16 in wide is not so very difficult, it is going to involve the constructor in some neat work with a scalpel, and if he proposes to fit a covering board, which runs round the edge of the deck, the planks will need to be joggled into it and this has got to be neatly done if it is to look reasonable. If you have seen a deck where the planks are properly joggled (for detail see Longridge) then planked decks where the planking simply runs out to the bulwarks will always jar. At least, they jar on me — I am perhaps being unreasonable about it. While on decks, I think (personally again) that the plank fastenings are perhaps best ignored. The bolt heads are usually covered with wooden plugs whose grain follows that of the plank and the result is not as 'dotty' as some planked model decks show up. I am not sure that this *is* a quibble, after all the impression of a deck is long, straight, thin black lines of caulking with the butt joints showing up as a pretty pattern.

The reason why I suggested a small supply of extra long planks is that Murphy's Law is applicable when planking a deck. Where a plank has to be joggled it will often be found that there should be a butt joint in the plank, usually a couple of feet away from the joggled end. While the rules of wooden shipbuilding were made to

be followed for satisfactory results, I don't think the shipwright would have actually *made* a butt joint so close to the end of a plank — he would sort through the pile for a long enough piece. Well, that's my theory and I'm stuck with it.

With our feet now planted on an impeccable deck the other items of *Number 12's* deck furniture are hatches, the boat, guns and sails. The guns are rolled up from sticky labels, the clever part here is getting the taper and diameters right. The ship's boat is stored upside down quite deliberately because it does show the clinker planking and it doesn't show the inside. Anyway, it is only a small boat and the spray doesn't lie in her if she is upside down.

I must say that I fiddled with sails for quite a while. I think it is necessary to mould them to a 3d shape, flat paper can never look like anything else. Finally I settled on Kleenex for Men using a small paint brush to wet the tissue (used double

i.e from the box) onto your mould. I don't know what you will use but I searched all over for a sufficiently large plastic pudding basin. The curvature of the mould needs to be such that you can wet enough tissue onto it to get out the sails you want without wrinkles. Hint — start in the middle and wet it circularly outwards using plenty of water. When you have plastered it down blot off excess water and use a *soft* half inch brush to put PVA glue, Resin W etc, all over it. The method is cheap so an experimental programme is not exactly prohibitive. To avoid the shine I gave my pudding basin a light grit-blast.

Attaching sails to masts and spars is not too easy. I reckon next time I shall have all fore and aft sails assembled on to masts and booms etc before the masts are stepped. Stiffening the sheets with glue is one method of holding (eg jibs) in place but I feel there must be a better way. If I find one I might let you know.

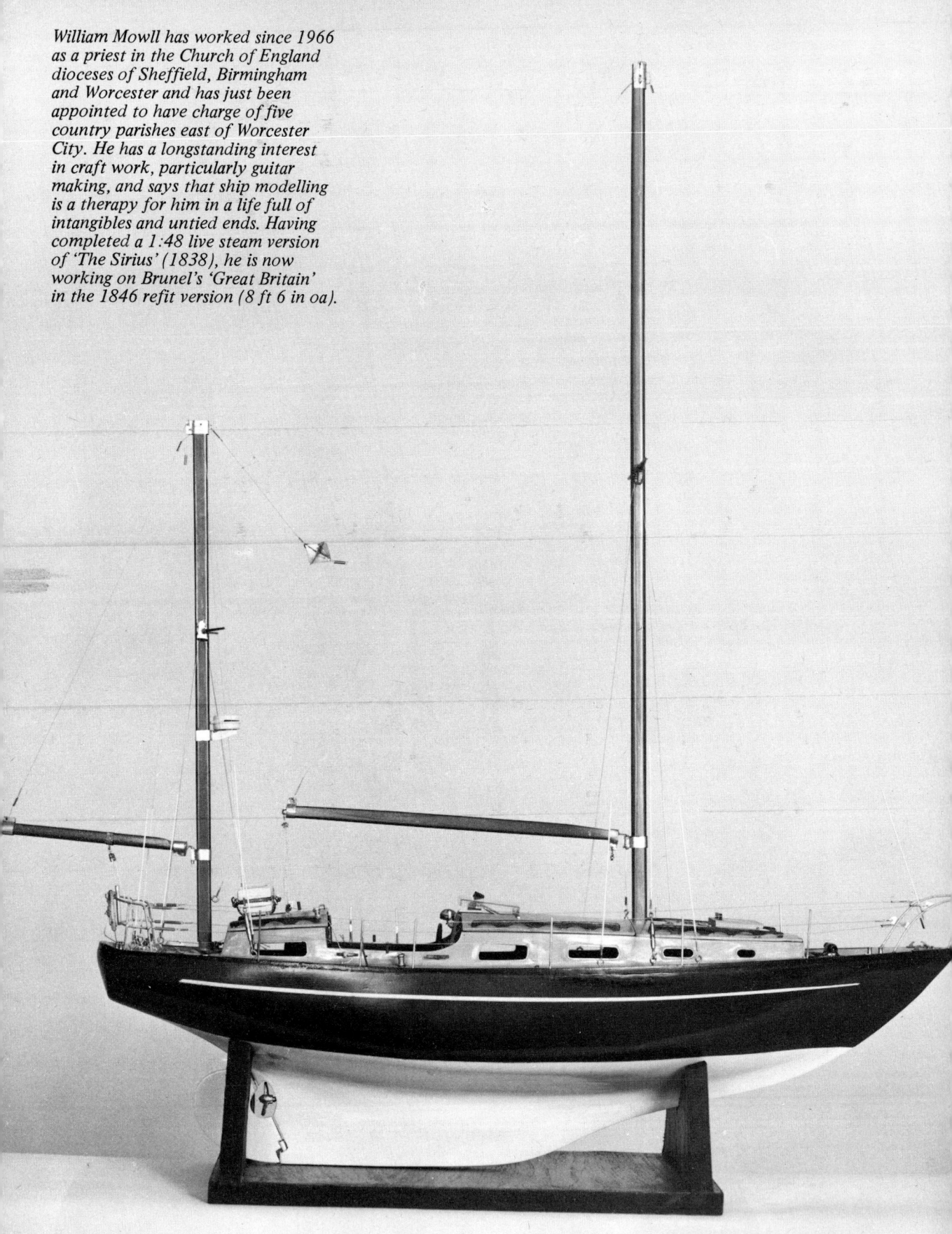

William Mowll has worked since 1966
as a priest in the Church of England
dioceses of Sheffield, Birmingham
and Worcester and has just been
appointed to have charge of five
country parishes east of Worcester
City. He has a longstanding interest
in craft work, particularly guitar
making, and says that ship modelling
is a therapy for him in a life full of
intangibles and untied ends. Having
completed a 1:48 live steam version
of 'The Sirius' (1838), he is now
working on Brunel's 'Great Britain'
in the 1846 refit version (8 ft 6 in oa).

A Nicholson 38

by William Mowll

The idea that a yacht should be a speed machine comes more easily to some than others. The *Nicholson 38* is a ketch of classic proportions for a medium sized luxury yacht with a slightly old-fashioned look which I would call graceful. An eminently sea-worthy yacht, with a pedigree in deep water sailing, it is a 'stiff' boat to handle and men's work to sail, but once under way the exhilarating feeling of riding through the swell, ploughing the foaming furrow in off-shore waters all contributes to the special joy of being at the helm of a boat built in the finest traditions of British boat yards by Camper & Nicholsons of Gosport.

This then, is a brief account of the way I set about building a model of a *Nicholson 38*, registered under the name *Samaria*, to a scale of ¾ in = 1 ft. Following the above fanfare of trumpets, let me hastily add that I am not in the same bracket of experience and my miniature replica is in fact the first scratch scale model boat that I have attempted, which may be of encouragement to some and possibly a source of annoyance to others who could have done better. My amateur craft background is in making acoustic guitars and there are, surprisingly, many similarities between the two skills although initially they appear to belong to two different worlds.

At the outset, not only did I know little about modelling ships, but I was also ignorant of the technicalities involved in the yachting world. To offset these yawning gaps in my knowledge, I was able to obtain some builder's plans which gave excellent exterior and interior details. My imagination was fired, and a throw away challenge by a friend that I should include all the plumbing was enough to make me reach out for the nearest piece of marine ply and switch on the bandsaw.

When I first saw the plans, my initial reaction was that the hull was rather too full in the waist to be really attractive, but as the boat progressed I had reason to modify my views. The rudder is a very important part of the aesthetics of the total hull, but as it is not added until a much later stage, one has a vague feeling of imbalance in the interim building period. The

Below: The cabin top removed to show some of the interior detail. Note the bedding on the after cabin bunk and the detail on the engine (below the model builder's nameplate).
All photos by courtesy of the author

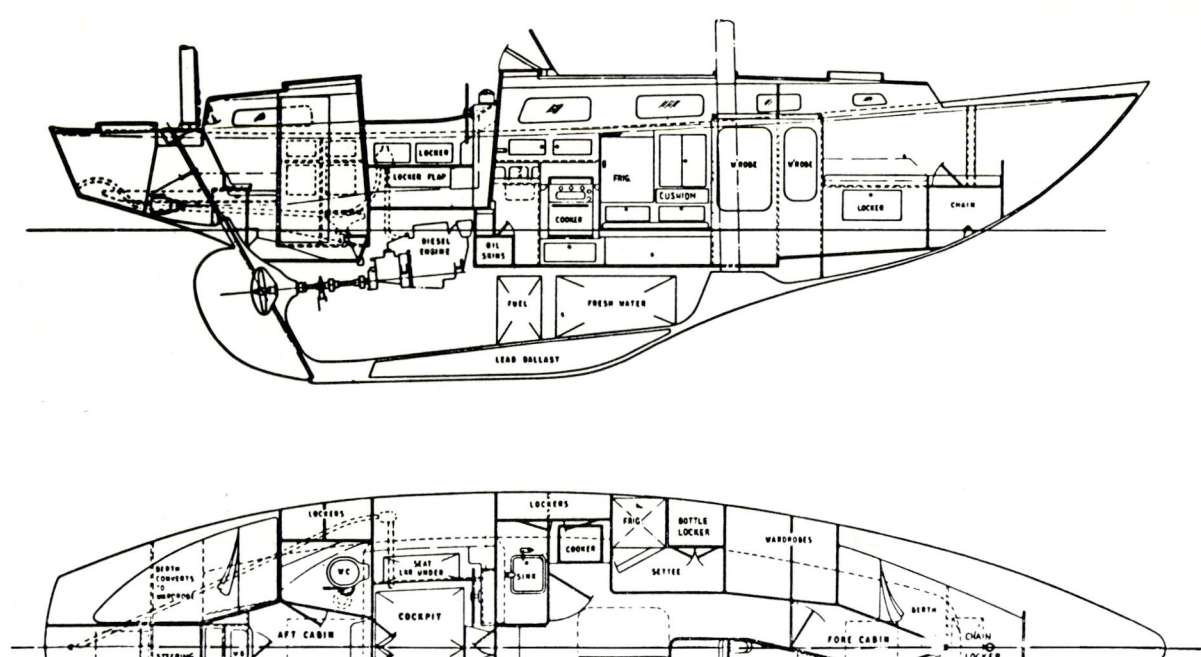

extended boom aft of the vessel adds length and a touch of elegance to the finished appearance.

I have a thorough dislike of fibreglass as a material and my heart goes out to all those craftsmen who have had to stomach the technological revolution in boat building which has meant the substitute of GRP and aluminium in place of teak, mahogany and spruce. But the *Nicholson 38* is obviously a GRP boat and as soon as my hull was planked over the bulkhead frames, on went a dilute solution of resin paste filler on both the exterior and the interior of the hull, completely covering the carvel laid mahogany planks and the sacrilege of making wood look like plastic was committed, accompanied by a murmuring resentment.

The prototype has lead ballast

built into the keel and this was followed in the model, although it needs relatively more. This was winged into the exterior and later packed on the interior to make the model float to the waterline, some 5 lb of lead in total. From childhood, I remember having a wartime toy presented to me by a lady in the WRNS. It was a solid waterline model of a destroyer and although I was pleased to have the toy, I was bitterly disappointed to discover that it would only float upside-down. I wondered how on earth we were supposed to win naval supremecy with a performance like that! I determined from then on that any model ship that I built would float in the conventional way and I have applied this to the *Nicholson,* even though it is really more for looking at than launching.

The hull finished, I gritted my teeth and used the dreaded fibreglass tissue for the decking around the cabins. At about the same time, I discovered in a major car accessory shop some peculiar silver tape with a diamond texture, which I cut up and used as the non-slip moulding impression so familiar on modern GRP craft. The result, when sprayed, looked remarkably authentic. The finish was, quite simply, car cellulose spray paints in the *Nicholson* colours of midnight blue contrasting with a pastel blue on the deck and cabin. The antifouling paint was Grecian white. The ribband was put on by slitting adhesive (masking) tape and letting the curvature of the hull open the slit, which was then sprayed, care being taken to protect the hull from overblow.

One of the problems for the

scale modeller working in a fairly large scale, is deciding how far one wants to get carried away. It is possible to make working locks on the doors, live gas jets on the gimbal stove and pressurized water in the plumbing, to say nothing of the marvels of proportional radio operation of such gadgets. To some extent I set my face against gimmicks, but was at the same time determined that the three cabins should have the atmosphere of places which are lived in. Whilst on the subject of authenticity, I try wherever it is possible to use original metals and materials. This applies as much to sink tops as it does to the eiderdown duvet covers in miniature flowered material. Such detail may appear pedantic, but the eye is a harsh task-master and able to detect false from true in hundredths of a second, to say nothing of hundredths of an inch.

A miniature library was made up from a convenient bargain book offer on the back of one of the Sunday colour supplement magazines. Alistair MacLean and a book on Opera stand shoulder to shoulder with *Everyman's Encyclopaedia* and *Hints on Gardening*. Because of the shelf sighting under the starboard

side decking it can only be seen by peering through the port-side cabin windows and is almost impossible to photograph successfully. I understand that model boats often have such secrets.

The section which has aroused most comment is surprisingly not the main cabin with its plush kitchen fitments, but the shower and heads next to the forward cabin. Although producing a scale lavatory is not a particularly difficult task, years of prudish suppression in the toy trade make this into an item of intense interest to both adults and children

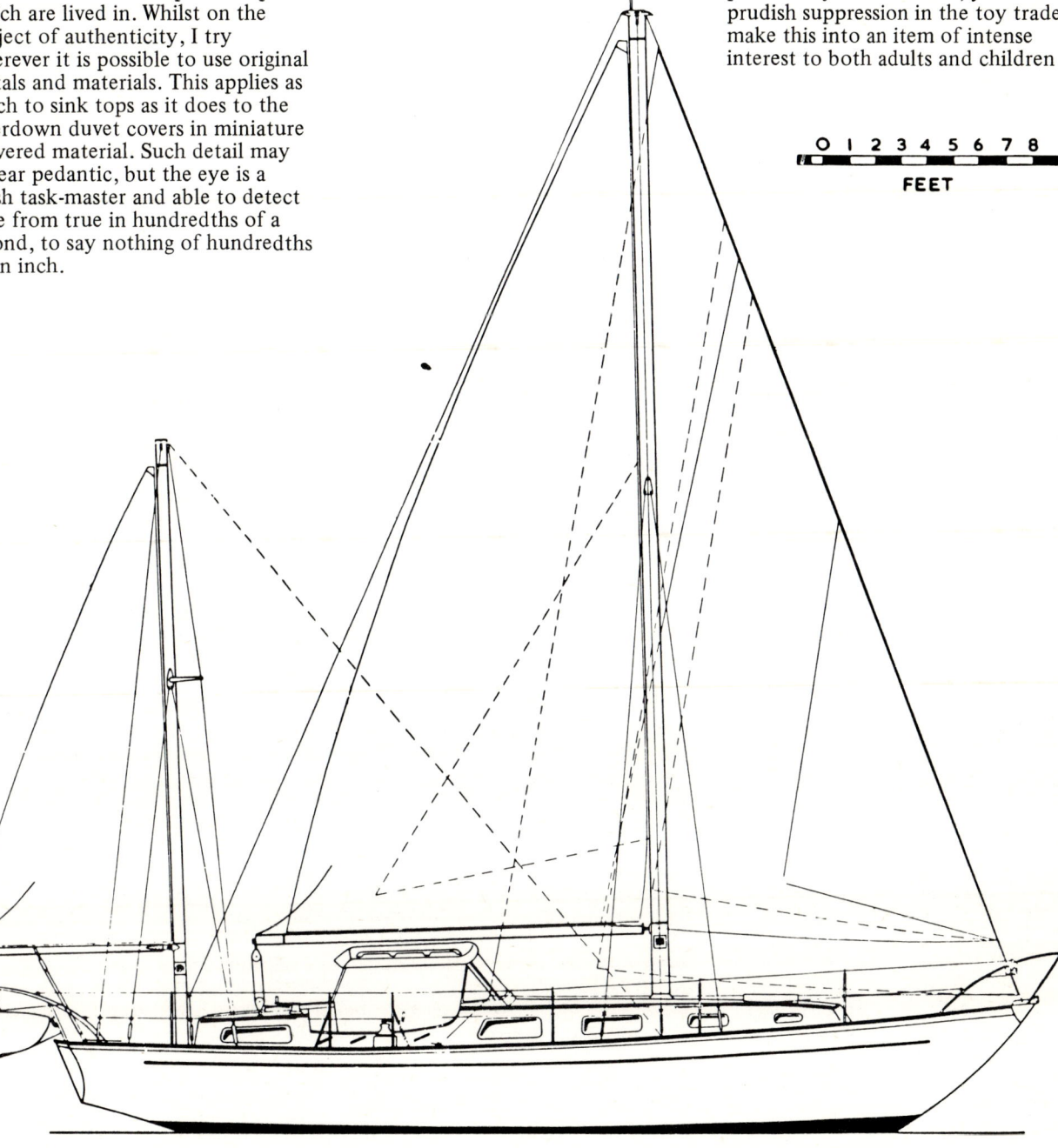

O 1 2 3 4 5 6 7 8
FEET

9

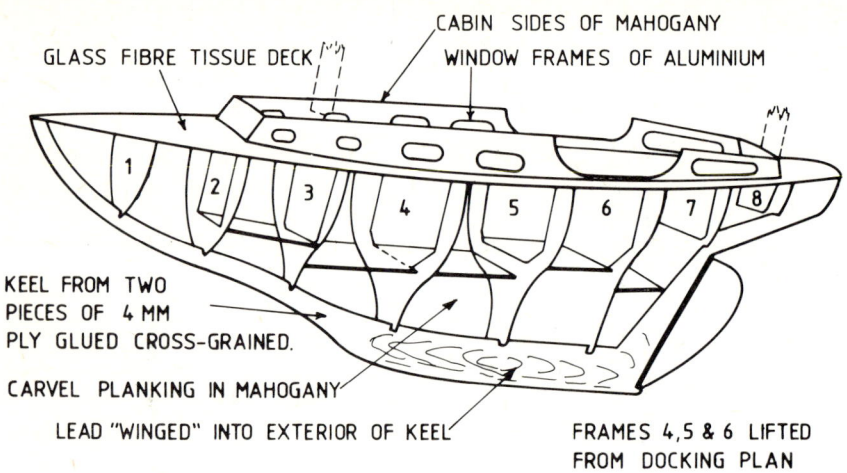

GLASS FIBRE TISSUE DECK

CABIN SIDES OF MAHOGANY
WINDOW FRAMES OF ALUMINIUM

KEEL FROM TWO
PIECES OF 4 MM
PLY GLUED CROSS-GRAINED.

CARVEL PLANKING IN MAHOGANY

LEAD "WINGED" INTO EXTERIOR OF KEEL

FRAMES 4,5 & 6 LIFTED
FROM DOCKING PLAN

DIAGRAMMATIC SKETCH OF CONSTRUCTION OF MODEL'S HULL

alike. The black plastic lid of the seat and the white pan (which is the top off a Smartie tube) with the little pump lever handle causes whoops of delight that this convenience should have been included on board. The adjacent basin does have a plughole and is made from a reduced razor blade dispenser, retaining that marvellous quartered edge, reminiscent of enamel-ware over a long period. The wash-basin in the after cabin, though smaller, is built into a vanity unit between the double bunk and the auxiliary bunk/hanging space.

There was a rhetorical question in my mind as to what I should do about the auxiliary engine. There was plenty of room for an electric motor and batteries and no real problems of fitting a working unit, but at the time I was feeling in a modelling mood rather than an engineering one and I decided that as this was basically a static model, I would build a mock up of a Perkins diesel engine, the standard fitment in this boat. I had the outline and I studied photographs in various yachting magazines. You would perhaps laugh if you knew that the crank-case was made out of a mint sweet dispenser and a pill box sawn down the middle. Added to this unlikely foundation were electrical carbon resistors, bits of tubing and pvc wire and a host of improbable bedfellows which together create an overall impression of a hefty diesel in miniature. Although it is only an illusory

dummy, the deception is quite powerful particularly as it is hidden beneath the cockpit floor and it makes an exciting discovery for anyone being taken on a tour of inspection round the boat.

In the cockpit, the steering wheel (the only proprietory item on the model) is connected to a guitar machine-head peg. The gearing on these string tensioners is at a ratio of approx 16:1. In order to make the rudder work in scale, I used a single connecting wire strand, fed through a tube on to the rudder arm, located under the lazaret. The rudder arm was offset with a tension spring so that when the wheel is spun in the cockpit, the tension tightens pulling the rudder from a full left hand turn through to a full right hand one in about 16 turns which is approx true to the prototype.

Other spin-offs from the guitar world are the piston hinges used on the main cockpit hatch cover, fabricated from a 'D' string inside a piece of small bore brass tube. This has the effect of allowing the hatch to stop exactly where it is positioned. Finally the ball ends of guitar strings are actually turned brass with a most convenient groove: these are pillaged for the working blocks of the running rigging. Still in the cockpit, the ship to shore radio plus miniature microphone sits underneath the radar screen, the logging lines provided by an inserted colour photograph. Likewise the aquatronic set on the cabin roof uses photographs of the appropriate dials, adding authenticity

to the navigational aids. The bowl head of the compass is fashioned from the top of a cheap screwdriver handle and set within a brass stabilizing ring. The realism of this is in the distorted optics one gets unless viewed from directly overhead. Really and truly it ought to work, but I had a lazy moment I guess.

Details is one thing, structure quite another. I knew that the cabin roofs were going to give me a rough ride — a beastly exacting job which might have to end up being made from a fibreglass mould. The main problems were curvature, which had to be absolutely correct, and they also had to be removable and therefore had to rely on their own inbuilt strength without warping or distorting. Even Nicholsons' did not have this problem with their single piece moulded deck. To worsen my difficulties it was necessary to cut the forward cabin and the main cabin roofs in order to gain access without having to remove the foremast. My previous experience in the 'bellying' of guitars has taught me to respect the often unknown and incalculable results of tensioning timber and yet I remain astounded by the possibilities of soaking and steaming wood round the old heated copper tube. My worst fears allayed, the curvature took easily enough and to stabilize it, I glued the two layers of 1/32 ply and clamped them up until dry. The pleasure of this little task completed was enhanced by the

I am indebted to Messrs Camper & Nicholsons Ltd, Gosport, Hants, for permission to reproduce the accompanying plans of the vessel.

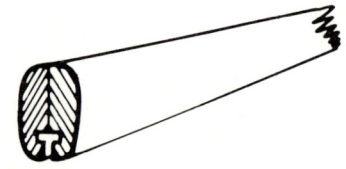

MASTS AND BOOMS HALVED, GROOVED AND REJOINED TO ACCOMMODATE SAILS AND STRENGTHEN AGAINST WARPING

knowledge that I had hoodwinked the evil smelling, mess-making, severely irritant fibreglass strand and resin from stinking the house out and making the butter taste distinctly peculiar!

Before taking a look at the rigging proper, a word about that stanchion rail. It was made from 1/16 in brass tubing and drilled through with a 1/32 in bit. In order to do this accurately and systematically I used a piece of tubing which sleeved over the 1/16th stanchion pre-drilling the holes and using it as a jig. Fed through the holes is that gorgeous stainless steel wire which the aeromodelling fraternity use as control lines to their stunt aircraft, immensely tough stranded stuff which has a marvellous will 'o the wisp appearance — sometimes you can see it and sometimes you cannot. Because of this last fact, I thought it a kindness to spring load the stanchion wire, so that accidental brushes against it are of no consequence as they are absorbed by the springs and the wires remain tight and smart looking. Finally the masts and booms were all split, grooved to form a 'T' section, re-glued and finished in bronzed aluminium paint spray. They were split not only because of the groove to accommodate the sails, if fitted, but also to prevent warping. Surprisingly, it also strengthens them.

The hook about model ships as far as I am concerned is their ability to be pieces of sculpture with which one can live. The completed ketch is aesthetically very pleasing and easy on the eye. The stubbiness of the hull is offset by the protruding boom and the pert prow passes with a graceful elegance to the full roundness of the rudder.

I am forever saying that model ships are not toys. Normally, I do not have the opportunity to go on to say that they are a disciplined art form which includes, in miniature, nearly all of the processes of building the real thing. Such models as this take about the same amount of time to complete at home as they would be scheduled for building on a boat yard basis, and I suspect that they give not only an equal portion of pleasure but also the much needed chance to dream awhile.

A RENDEL GUNBOAT

HMS FIDGET

by Ray Cattle

This article ought to have been sub-titled 'How to get 'sent' by a gunboat!' But as circumstances would later prove, I had not exactly picked an easy task in my choice of model. Problems were legion and at one stage, with over 75 per cent of the work completed, they appeared insurmountable. To start at the beginning, I had purchased a small publication entitled *British Warships 1845-1945* from the bookstall at the Science Museum, London. Leafing through its twenty pages my attention was drawn to a faintly ridiculous craft, the model of which (HMS *Arrow*) I had overlooked on my trip to the Museum. Though not quite love at first sight, the quaint concept and Victorian thinking obvious behind the construction more than interested me. The ultimate in diplomacy, the big gun, pointed its 10inch bore straight over the bow; jingoism pure and simple — the substance of immediate appeal to this modeller.

HISTORY

The invention of these floating gun carriages had, with due precedent, necessity as an anxious parent. The firm of W G Armstrong & Co were by local pressure being denied the use of their firing range at Whitley Sands. To surmount the objections and in solution to the problem an experimental test firing took place at sea, the barrel to be proved being mounted aboard a barge, thereby effectively pointing the way to an entirely new era in naval construction. *Staunch* was the first 'Rendel', after the designer and innovator Mr (later Sir) George Wightwick Rendel. Launched from Armstrong's yard at Newcastle into the Tyne in 1867, she arrived opportune to the philosophy of the age. Britain was then in the throes of fortress mania and the little craft, with the advantages of low cost and expendability, exactly suited the defence requirement. Such bargain basement power also interested foreign admiralties and many vessels were to be produced under licence; from such beginnings great empires are founded. The current combine known as Vickers Armstrong Ltd owes much to the insignificant gunboat.

Fidget, launched from Chatham Dockyard in 1873, cost the tax-paying public the modest sum of £9006 (equivalent to £105.95 per foot). She survived as an effective unit till hulked as yard craft *C21* in 1905 and finally went as scrap in 1920. This longevity was a common factor with her class, indeed there is just an outside chance that one still exists. *Cuckoo*, also launched in 1873, was last heard of at Plymouth in 1959. Reduced to a hulk *(YC 37)* since 1923, she may still be afloat as a dumb barge somewhere and any information that can be provided as to her present whereabouts, or ultimate fate, would be appreciated.

Reference must be made to the curious use of names for the class. Normally one can trace some connection, some common descent between the names and indeed the name ship *(Ant)* usually is homogenous to the rest, but a check on those used discloses an odd

mixture from heavenly bodies (*Comet*), through ornithology (*Kite, Bustard* and *Cuckoo*), into mammals (*Bloodhound, Mastiff, Bulldog, Badger, Weazel* and *Hyaena*), fish (*Pike*), reptiles (*Snake*), weapons (*Arrow*) and finally an ill assortment of absurdities (*Fidget, Pickle, Snap, Scourge, Blazer* and *Bonetta*) — what is a Bonetta? (Another word for bonito, the striped tunny, a large mackerel type fish. **Editor**).

I can recommend for further study R M Anderson's excellent article in *Warship International* (Vol I 1976) and the earlier, more general, book by Preston and Major entitled *Send a Gunboat*.

THE HULL

The plans for *Fidget* were obtained via the good offices of the National Maritime Museum, Greenwich and in particular with the kind help of David Lyon MA, to whom I wish to extend my grateful thanks. Luckily for my finances the details were contained on two sheets only which, although expensive, did not quite cripple. (It seems a pity that Her Majesty's Stationery Office should levy such a punitive price on this aspect of their services as I am sure than an increase in business would follow a reduction in charges and more than compensate for any loss in revenue.) Due to the physical size of the model and the desire to install radio control I decided to produce the hull from glass fibre. This, while answering the internal space requirement, also provided the possibility of further models from

Ray Cattle first took up ship modelling seriously some five years ago, and his main interest lies in the construction of scale working models. He is particularly attached to naval vessels of the Victorian period, and adds that the more unusual they are in build or appearance the more attractive they become as possible subjects for a model.

Below: HMS *Fidget* under way; note the low freeboard
Photo by John Bowen

the same mould, *Fidget* having nineteen sisters.

With the advantages understood and the disadvantages as yet unrealised, I began work on the plug, which I made from ordinary soft wood, laid up to the hull's lines in the the usual way. Not being familiar with the techniques and practices of glass fibre I made it my business to study every book and pamphlet I was able to secure. Armed with all this theoretical knowledge, plus the helpful hints and sometimes downright unhelpful suggestions of my acquaintances, I bravely put

everything to one side for about two months!

Guilt and a growing concern that the sap in the cheap wood could cause problems finally drove me back to the project. With much recourse to notes (which tended to stick to my fingers anyway), I proceeded to 'lay up' the glass fibre mould. Something worthy of mention if only in caution. I had included the the rubbing strake and foredeck as part of the mould pattern — a mistake; being projections these caused many problems, not the least of which was the difficulty in

separating the pattern from the mould. The execution of this was not without loss of blood, and came as near to brute force and ignorance as makes no matter. However, as it is not my intention to write a definitive article on the trials and tribulations of GRP (or the use of the tourniquet for the home handyman), I will draw a veil over the rest of this episode and request the reader to assume the hull finished, in so far as any imperfections have been filled and a coat of primer applied.

Wishing to imitate the plating of the hull, I used gum paper in *appliqué* and assured complete adhesion with a coat of varnish; this is best carried out while the 'plates' are still damp rather than risk their rejection when the gum dries out. Gum paper as a material tends to be 'hairy' but care with sealing and rubbing down will eventually produce a flat finish.

I also completely 'riveted' the hull the rivet points being formed from droplets of white glue applied by means of a hypodermic syringe, the needle of which for safety's sake was 'disarmed' with the removal of its point. My decision to model the plate fastenings unfortunately seems to have become a matter for some controversy. The vessel's specification lists the method employed as 'countersunk' (which just goes to prove you should always read the specification, preferably before building the model). However, the working is 'countersunk', not 'flush', therefore I am going to place my defence on the fact that although 'flush' riveting must also be 'countersunk' the reverse is not always the case, as during this period in ship construction the points were not automatically ground off.

RUDDER AND PROPELLERS

I made the rudder from one piece of sheet brass, the shaft being filed to shape. The upper pivot has the benefit of a ball race and the servo linkage, all carefully assembled and checked — care that knowledge of later inaccessibility brings.

The four-bladed propellers were easier to produce than I at first thought possible, due to the relative simplicity of the blade shape. Also, as a bonus, they have proved more efficient in moving the model than those available commercially. I used soft solder in conjunction with my method of taper pegging the blade to the boss. The taper provides for initial rigidity, enabling the propellers to be set up by eye before running in the solder. I did not consider a jig necessary as the diameters were small. In keeping with normal practice the propellers are set 'handed' and operate contra-rotating.

After deciding on the location of the radio's main components I cut a false deck (with access hatches) structurally stiffened for strength and to form the deck camber. When installed, I gave the surface a coat of black paint followed by strips of Rollwood as an overlay. This product combines a genuine wood veneer with a foil backing, thereby providing a greater flexibility and a more forgiving nature than the purely natural material. The caulking I simulated with tolerable success by the slight excess of glue and the pre-blackened 'under deck'.

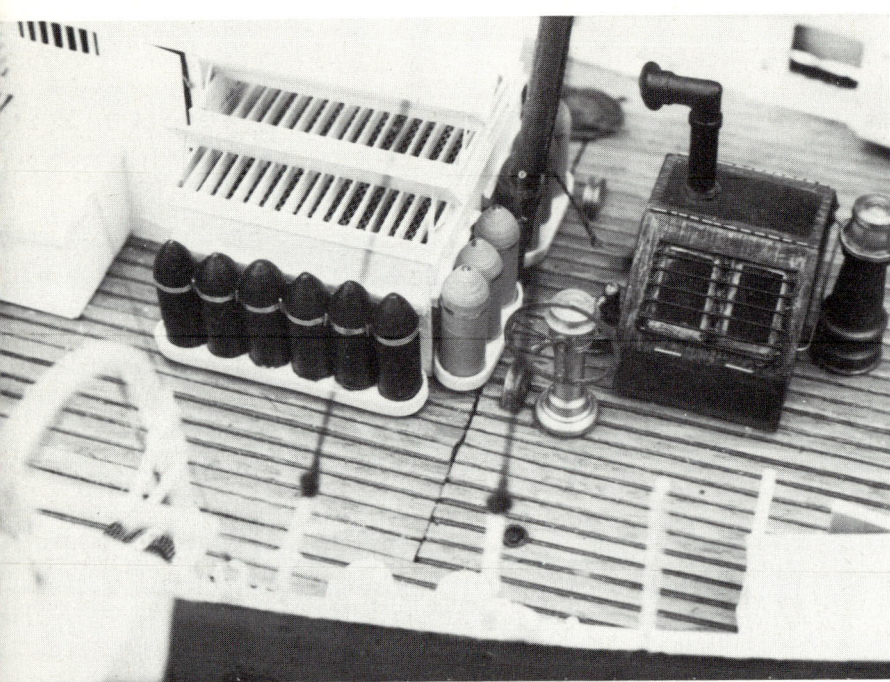

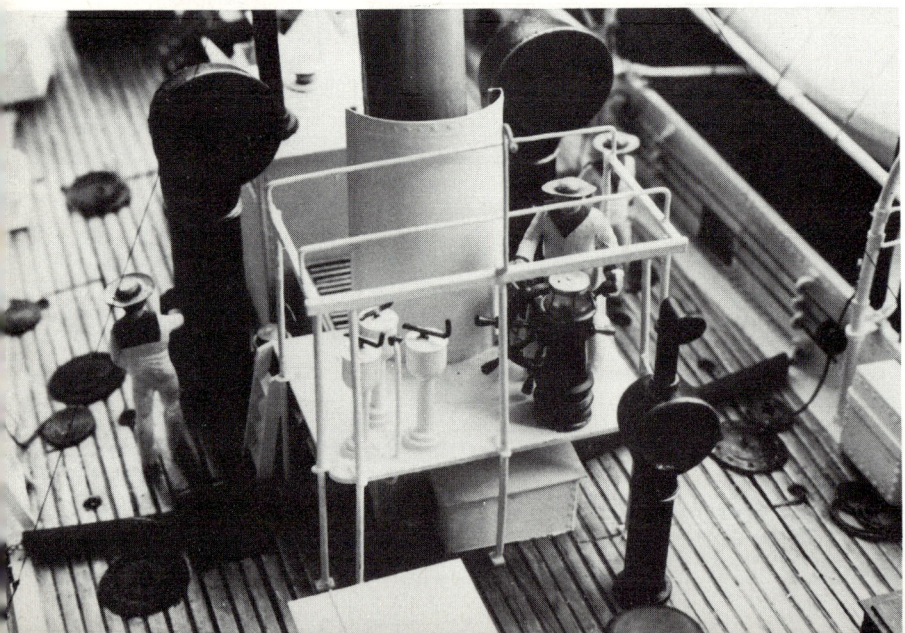

With a mind to past experiences and to prevent the situation most modellers detest I decided to work from one end of the model to the other, without deviation. This, I hoped, would provide a balanced work load rather than the normal problem of 'all the interesting bits done and only the repetitious and difficult left'.

I made use of a variety of materials in the construction of the upperworks, notable amongst which was plastic card, which is obtainable in several thicknesses and is convenient and clean in use. However, care must be taken to protect the finished article from undue heat or exposure to the sun's rays; also it is more than advisable to stiffen or completely block out the part with balsa (or similar) to prevent distortions in the unsupported areas. Due to my growing doubts as to the stability of this material I have now switched to another medium which, although not quite as convenient, has one overriding advantage — I can get any amount of it free! I refer to printer's litho plates which being of thin, pure aluminium are ideal for the modeller (the more so since the advent of these new Cyanoacrylate glues). The material has many points in its favour, not the least of which is the saving in weight over plastic, and of course a virtual guarantee of stability against chemical breakdown, providing the metal is protected by a coat of paint.

The main boiler room cowl vents are in themselves a testimony to the diverse use of modelling materials — steel washers, plastic tube, brass wire, brass rod, white glue and fibre reinforced modelling clay, combine to produce these features. The latter substance self hardens as the moisture evaporates and in its finished form is surprisingly light and strong. The vents double as the boiler room ash shoots, therefore doors have been cut into the plastic tube and, to display their presence, have been left open. Hinges and latches of litho were applied, with the paint, and the probable construction seams (of the cowl) followed with 'rivets' of white glue. The other cowl vent also had a combined function, that of vent to the auxiliary boiler room

Opposite, top: A close up of the skylight with its stove funnel, of the 4½ in deck pump and of the shells stowed in their racks.

Opposite, bottom: The steering position, with compass on top of the steering wheel standard and telegraphs alongside. Note the protective heat shield round the fore side of the funnel. The auxiliary boiler room vent and stove flue are just forward of the helmsman's position.

Below, top: The riveted construction of the main boiler room vents can be seen, as can the hinge at the base of the funnel. Note the ship's bell hung on the after side of the boiler room entrance.

Below, bottom: A general view looking down on the vessel, showing the amount of detail on this model. The black line running across the deck from the steering position is the cover over the steering chains, and the black disc just forward of this cover is a coaling scuttle.

Photos by courtesy of the author

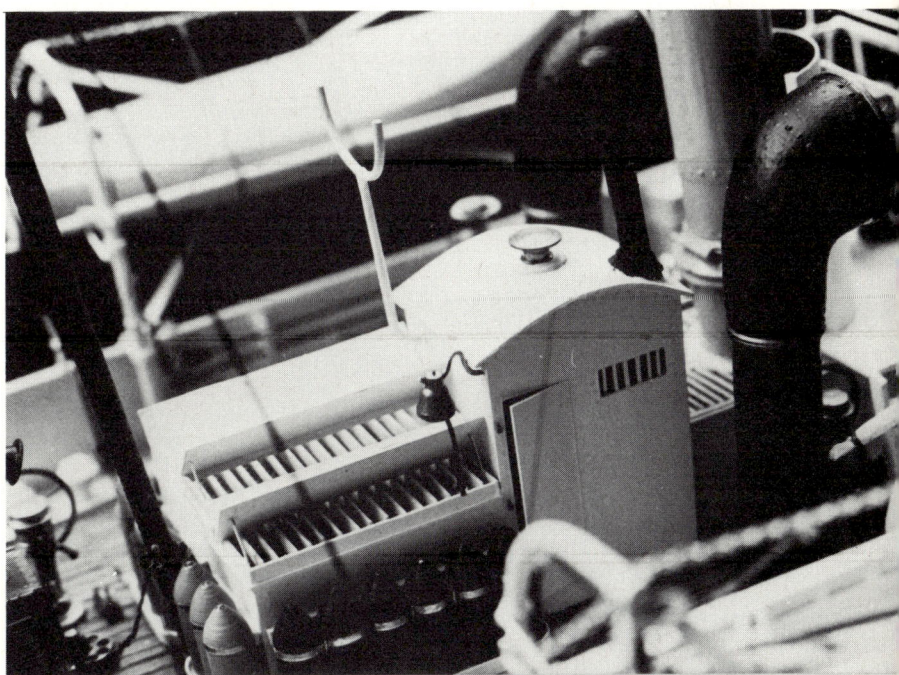

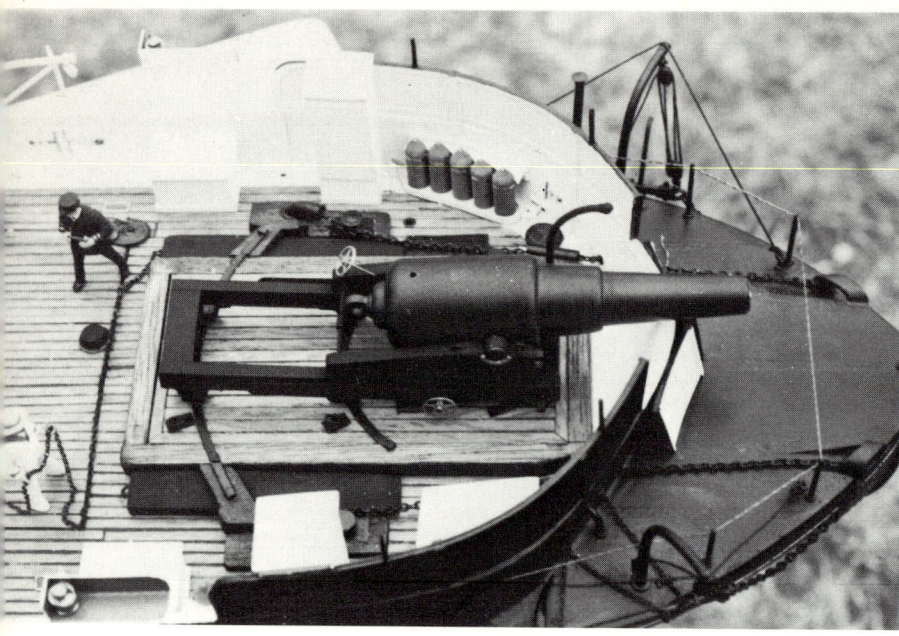

The 10inch muzzle loading gun on its carriage and platform; note the traversing rails. Also to be seen are the heads, the navigation lights, the anchor cables running to the chain pipes, the anchor davits and the shell stowage racks.
Photo by John Bowen

and support to the flue of a heating stove. Due to this parasitic chimney the cowl has a marked pot-bellied look and was simple to fabricate, being made from the handle of an old screwdriver, and a few minutes on the lathe.

FUNNEL AND GUN
Sometimes luck plays a part in the building programme! I had run out of solder and in picking up a new supply also effectively purchased *Fidget's* funnel, the solder's alloy container being the correct diameter. Again glue 'rivets' follow the construction seams and a hinge and latch system, modelled in deference to the fact that the funnel could be lowered, were added to the assembly.

Concealed within my bargain funnel and soldered to a length of brass tube is the upper end of the radio aerial. It is my opinion that the aerial position should be pinpointed as early as possible, to allow the site the best advantages of height and disguise the model can offer. There is nothing sadder than to see an otherwise excellent model ruined by the obvious piece of trailing wire, often found ostentatiously fixed to the masthead or some other prominent feature — a totally unnecessary concession to reception. Providing the majority of the aerial is above the water line its presence

outside the superstructure will not greatly improve the range, certainly not to the same degree that it is a depreciation to scale appearance.

I turned the gun from solid aluminium which, when lightly sprayed with Humbrol 'Hull Black', has the sheen and metal solidity present in contemporary photographs of this type of weapon. Elizabeth Castle on the island of Jersey has two examples of Armstrong muzzle loaders, and I was able to obtain details of rifling, proof marks, Victorian crest and elevation gradations from them. The size mounted by *Fidget* and most of her sisters were 10inch 18 tonners, truly an awesome piece when it is considered that this was one of the largest calibres then in service.

The binnacle stands I turned from brass, the tops from perspex, capped with brass, and used floral wire for the glazing bars, which for cleanliness were 'glued' in with matt varnish.

The wheels needed for the 4½ in deck pumps I adapted from scrapped pocket watch parts. The decoration to the pump head I achieved by allowing the lathe tool to 'chatter' on the turning. This 'sunburst' effect also found its use in ornamenting the gun's muzzle plug.

The dividing head and division plate I have as accessories for my Unimat lathe made life easy in the

production of the two spool-like distribution heads for the deck pumps, the spoke location points on the ship's wheel, and similarly the propeller blade pre-station holes.

Due to the scale of the model (¼ in = 1 ft) I found it necessary to put considerable effort into the construction of the various deck fittings, modelling to detail rather than just an indication. Accordingly I am indepted to the excellent drawings of the late Norman A Ough as they provided the source material from which the radial davits, boat anchors and watertight hatch details were drawn.

A feature of the model which tends not to be noticed is the studs to the anchor cable. This I achieved, at great risk to eyesight (and bankruptcy to the swear box) by the introduction of tiny pieces of brass floral wire across each link. I stretched the chain taut over the work surface and positioned a piece of white card beneath; this helps prevent your eyes becoming too crossed and makes finding the 'studs' easy when dropped, a frequent occurrence! Humbrol 'Hull Black' was again used, in part as a fixing medium. I have twice made reference to this particular paint as I feel the slight sheen which the colour imparts has an advantage to this scale of model over purely matt paint.

In concession to the habit of the age of sail, the 'heads' were sited forward, and to either side of the gun mounting. The officers' WC (port) had the convenience of a lift pump, external to the structure. The ratings, however, were provided with a curious

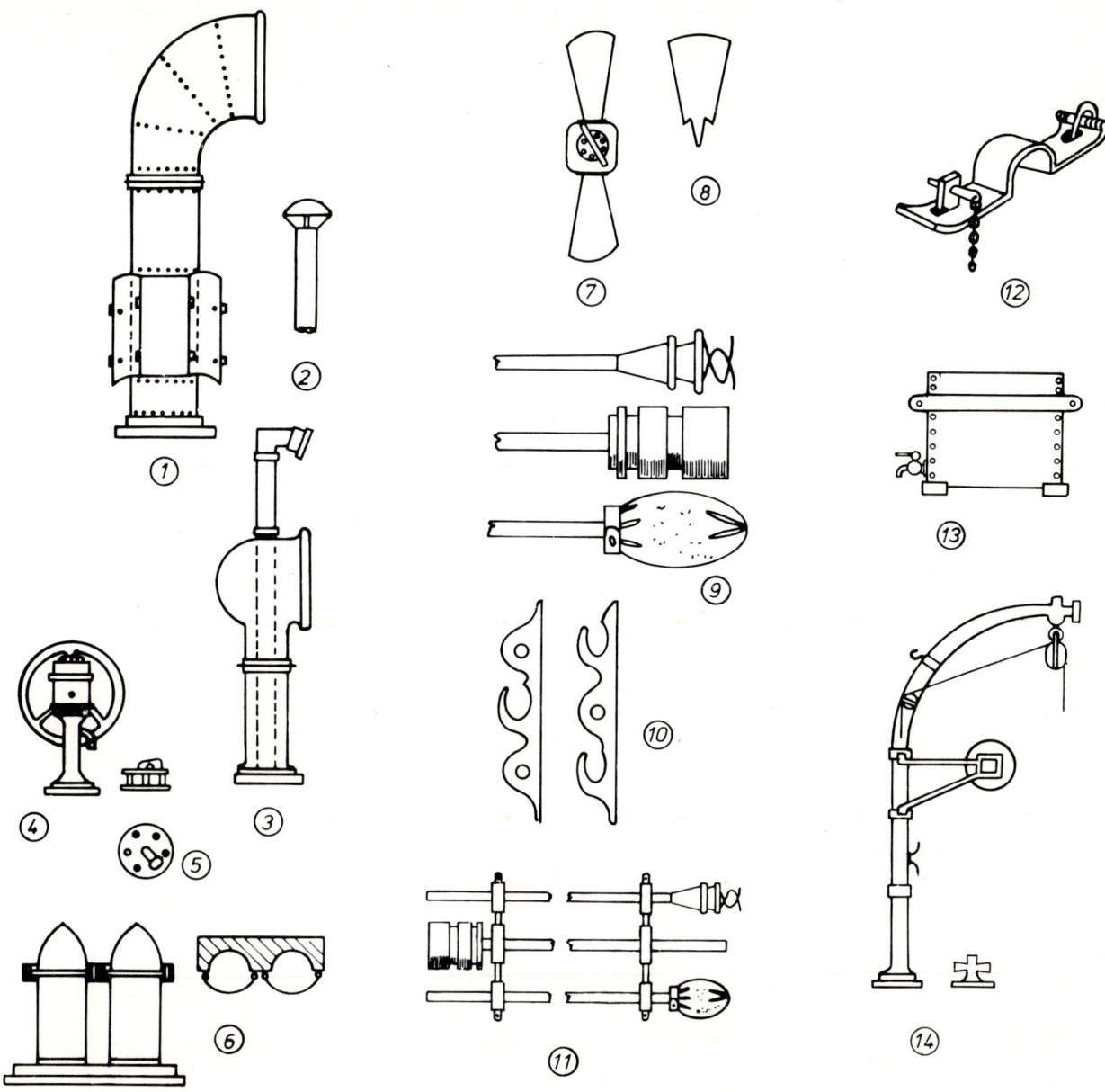

①	MAIN BOILER ROOM COWL VENT & ASH SHOOT	⑧	TAPER PEG BLADE
②	GALLEY FUNNEL	⑨	RAMMERS, ETC
③	AUXILIARY BOILER ROOM VENT & STOVE FLUE	⑩	RACK DETAIL
④	4 1/2" DECK PUMP & DISTRIBUTOR HEAD	⑪	RAMMER RACK & METHOD OF STOWAGE
⑤	PLAN VIEW OF DISTRIBUTOR HEAD	⑫	TRUNNION PLATE
⑥	SHELL RACK	⑬	WATER TANK
⑦	PROPELLER	⑭	RADIAL DAVIT & STAGHORN BOLLARD

basin external to theirs, the purpose of which would appear to have been a combination of urinal and manual sea water flush system. *Fidget* being built in 1873 had the benefit of splinter proof 'offices', while her earlier sisters had to make do with mere canvas dodgers — and presumably draughts!

WEIGHT SAVING

But long before this the problem I hinted at earlier had become manifest: the model was much too heavy. Not being familiar with the strength of glass fibre I had inbuilt the weight problem by using too much resin and a second layer of matt where, as it transpired, I need only have used one. From this realisation every effort was made to lighten ship, racks of shells are indeed shells, each being drilled hollow. The gun, on which so much care and attention had been lavished, was reduced by drilling and chiselling the underside metal away, and with this went my hopes of making the thing operational. These and other attempts at fining the weight down were unfortunately all to no avail, I was soon back looking for new areas of weight savings.

Next to receive such attention was the functional side. Five batteries totalling 6 volt at 1.8 amp had been provided; these were exchanged for four at 1.2 amp, this reduction in voltage and physical size made a considerable weight loss. Accordingly work was resumed but horror of horrors, despite every care and economy these hard won ounces were soon eroded. With the gunboat down on its load water line and some four ounces of modelling still to be allowed for, despair set in. I felt as though the project was doomed and that I was about to become a 'static' modeller — not the worst of fates I know, but near enough, for a radio control enthusiast. Salvation came with a friend's suggestion that the radio's requirements could be coupled with that of the main power source, and the radio's battery pack removed. Viability at a price, but the endurance is adequate for the normal regatta. I say normal, for unfortunately I failed to have enough 'steam' to complete the circumnavigation of the Round Pond

Above: The shallow hull of these vessels is clearly seen here, as is the 'riveted' construction of the hull. Note the lead of the anchor cable through the fairleads on the deck edge to the anchors stowed on deck under the anchor davits.

in Kensington Gardens earlier this year. But in scaled up distance I doubt the full-sized vessel would have had sufficient bunkerage either.

The dinghy I made by use of an injection technique. A balsa plug of the hull shape was made, minus keel, and a female mould cut from a piece of scrap wood. With the mould suitably blocked up, to give clearance beneath, the opening was covered with a piece of plastic card and heated under the cooker grill. When the plastic softened the plug was gently eased through. After trimming, the resultant shape was fitted out with keel etcetera, then completely planked, internally and

externally using thin plastic strip. With bottom boards, rowlocks and all other necessities the boat was judged ready for painting and hanging on the davits. The gig, however, was made covered, not through laziness on my part but as a further offering to the weight problem. The savings I had made all came from the fore part of the vessel and as the dinghy, in completed form proved to be no feather weight it was necessary to keep the gig as light as possible.

DETAILS

HMS *Fidget:* 254 tons displacement. 85 ft between perpendiculars, 26 ft 1 in beam, 6 ft 3 in depth. Crew: 25. Engines: 110 NHP/180 to 270 ihp: 7.5 to 8.7 kts. Coal 20 to 35 tons. One 10inch mlr. Shell weight 406 lb. Muzzle velocity 1379 ft per sec. Approximate penetration, iron armour 12 in.

Restoring Prisoner-of-War Models

by Jonathan Tatlow

As a modelmaker I served my apprenticeship with my brother at the best of all schools — our father's elbow. An incessant amateur, he filled our bleak war-time childhood with a succession of toys and models which were the envy of our less fortunate friends. Going further back in the family, my brass-bound mahogany handled carving chisels are all marked with the initials 'EW' — my great grandfather Edmund Whitaker. Throughout my boyhood models and modelling were an integral part of everyday life — and this was before the days of plastic assembly kits and at a time when materials of almost any sort were unobtainable, forcing upon us the invaluable attributes of salvage and ingenuity.

After training as a graphic designer I joined the staff of the leading antiques magazine *The Connoisseur* and a chance remark about a ship-in-a-bottle that I was mending for friends led to my being offered an antique model to restore for a West End dealer. Since then ship models in need of repair have continued to appear on the horizon, the most frequent being those made of bone by prisoners-of-war in Nelson's time.

A fully restored bone prisoner-of-war model of a 16-gun ship-rigged sloop, 14 in long, on its original stand. The model has a solid wood hull with brass pinned planks over, is flush decked with steering lines rigged from the open tiller to the steering wheel drum. Anchors, chainplates, pintles and gudgeons are of brass; guns, carriages, blocks and deadeyes are bone. The transom is finely carved and the figurehead shows a woman holding aloft — with wry humour — the Torch of Liberty.

HISTORICAL BACKGROUND

Most bone ship models were made by prisoners confined in this country during the Napoleonic Wars, which lasted virtually unbroken from 1793 until the Battle of Waterloo in 1815. By international agreement the prisoners were given a reasonable allowance of food but corruption amongst the staff and a high incidence of gambling amongst the inmates ensured that many of the men received little more than survival rations. Predictably, the more resourceful prisoners sought ways by which they could ease their conditions, or even put by enough money to facilitate an escape.

In contrast to the infamous English 'press gangs' the French used a system of nationwide conscription to man their armies and ships, and it can therefore be assumed that among the thousands of men captured there would have been a number of highly skilled craftsmen such as cabinet makers, watchmakers, carvers of wood and ivory, toolmakers and jewellers. These men began to search for ways in which they could adapt their skills to their grim surroundings.

At first the only materials available to them would have been scrap timber from firewood stacks and workshops, bones from the cookhouse and straw from the stables — and presumably tools would have been limited to small knives, razors and needles. But from these humble beginnings there developed a prolific and amazingly ingenious industry, so that regular and officially sanctioned markets began to be held in the prison yards, enabling the prisoners to trade their toys, models and knick-knacks with the local population.

A considerable amount of 'prisoner-of-war work' is preserved in museums and private collections, but it is the ship models that command the greatest interest. Built of either wood or bone, or a combination of the two, they vary from a few inches to several feet in length and depict almost any type of naval vessel, but the most frequently encountered are bone two and three deckers of, say, 74 to 90 guns, about twelve inches long overall.

Perhaps their size reflects the conditions under which they were made, being small enough to permit safe work and storage in a crowded blockhouse, but large enough to suit simple tools and the lack of proper workshop facilities. On the other hand, the profusion of models of that size might be the result of a compromise between producing an acceptably large ornament and an economic use of materials.

CONSTRUCTION

Plank-on-frame models are not unknown, but the usual method was to start with a carved wooded 'core'

to the lower hull to which the keel, stem and stern posts, planking, decking and upperworks were added in bone, glued and pinned in position. Ivory is not common, though it sometimes appears in miniatures, ships' boats and in fancy work at the bow and stern. Bone guns are not unusual but more often they have been roughly turned or filed from brass, whilst masts and spars are always of bone. Paintwork is minimal and usually confined to red undersides to gunport lids, figureheads and stern galleries picked out in red and black (and sometimes

Left: The bone model (shown on the previous page) stripped down and cleaned. The jibboom and spanker boom were both broken and the whole model had been crushed from above, breaking all three topgallant masts and ramming down the main and mizzen topmasts through the tops. All the yards that remained have been removed, as have all deck fittings, the few remaining guns, the boat and rudder. Flag-like identification labels can be seen attached to some parts of the rigging.
Below: A stern view of the model fully restored, a fifty pence coin indicating the intricacy of the work involved on such a scale.
Photos from the author's collection.

a pale apple green), and gold foil paper is sometimes used to good effect. The rigging is made of, or made up from, twine, cotton or silk, and in some cases human hair, with bone blocks and deadeyes.

Some models have a pair of draw strings protruding from under the transom, usually terminating in a bone bead. When pulled these triggered a simple mechanism concealed under the deck, causing all the guns to spring out simultaneously at the ports.

It is generally assumed that the production of the models was a communal activity involving a group or groups of relatively specialised workers. A man who could concoct a lathe of some sort would obviously be in high demand; a skilled carver would be kept busy producing figureheads and fretted stern galleries; whilst some would prefer hull work and others rigging. Considering the conditions under which they were made, the craftsmanship and detailing of prisoner-of-war models is remarkable and sometimes astounding, and in common with all 'sailor built' models they have a certain salty authenticity due to the simple fact that many of the men were modelling direct from their own experience.

Of the men who made the models very few names are now known. In his excellent book on the subject Ewart C Freeston cities a dozen names or so and I can only add one more to the list. While dismantling an ornate wood and straw work box lined with mirrors and housing a miniature two decker I discovered fragments of a letter and envelope. The envelope was addressed in spidery copperplate handwriting to 'Monsieur Morèbe, Prisonnier de Guerre' at a private address in Staffordshire, but only the last part of the letter was present, showing the closing words 'Liverpool 1801'. Presumably M Morèbe was on parole (there being no prison at the address shown) and one wonders whether the letter came from a less fortunate comrade in the prison at Liverpool.

The occasional naming of the ships is notoriously inaccurate but with good reason, historically speaking. In those pre-photography days, if news had just come through of a naval engagement favourable to their captors one can hardly blame the prisoners for hastily applying the name of the victorious vessel to a newly completed model in time for the next market, regardless of accuracy. I once restored a model proudly displaying the name *Leander* across her transom, but there the resemblance to any ship of that name ended. The reason for this 'deception' was that the model had originally been bought by crew members of the *Leander* for presentation to their captain, whose descendants enjoy it to this day.

RESTORATION

Diagnosis The golden rule is: never rely on memory. With this in mind a systematic survey is first made of all damage, the sole object being to record the model *as it is*, regardless of inaccuracies, so that after cleaning and repair every single item on the hull, on the masts and in the rigging can be re- assembled or replaced exactly as it was originally. From stem to stern and from keel to truck every broken, displaced or missing item is identified and carefully noted. A diagrammatic deck plan is made, sketches of the bow and stern areas are usually necessary, if only for colour notes, and the complexities of rigging details have necessitated the invention of a simple shorthand so that the run of a rope 'from yard arm to pin rail' can be written down with complete accuracy in a line or so.

As might be expected the most usual areas of damage are at the extremities: broken jibbooms, topgallant masts and spanker booms and their attendant rigging. And if the stand is broken or missing the model will have fallen on its beam ends, perhaps displacing the lower yards and certainly damaging their rigging. The failure of the original bone glue over the years results in displacement and losses amongst the guns, their bone carriages and other small deck fittings, and when the ship is viewed end-on it is often found that the mast caps and tops have become loose, allowing the three sections of the masts to fall out of alignment or to sag into a limp zig-zag. In the worst cases a model

may have lain for years in an attic unheeded and unprotected, to emerge a true wreck.

Stripping Down Starting at the jibboom end and working aft, all damaged and loose parts are removed, labelled and stored. In practice this generally entails the removal of almost all deck fittings and even sections of the bulwarks for re-placement, re-fixing or easier cleaning of the decks. Samples of rigging are kept to enable a perfect match to be made later on, and at this stage it usually becomes apparent that more work is required than might have been thought at first. For instance, if the jibboom has snapped at the bowsprit cap (a common occurrence) it will be necessary to remove almost all the rigging forward of the foremast, and although with care much can be stored intact or left hanging from the mast, the finer threads will be extremely brittle due to age and the unavoidable disturbance will inevitably lead to further breakages.

Sometimes it is necessary to remove an entire mast assembly in one piece and this is done by first disconnecting all stays and braces and any running rigging which falls to the deck and then slicing through the lower deadeye lanyards so that the whole 'Christmas tree' assembly can be lifted from its socket in the deck. However, this procedure is not normally necessary and to do so merely to gain convenient access to the decks would cause too much destruction of contemporary rigging.

The fixing of all blocks, bitts and channels in their respective positions

is thoroughly tested to ensure that they will withstand the strain of re-rigging, since it is obviously better to find any weak spots at this early stage. During the stripping down process the work of earlier restorers is sometimes revealed — often of a very poor standard and leading to further work.

Cleaning A model usually requires restoration because it has had no case, therefore the next task is the removal of the accumulated dirt of years. Gentle scrubbing with old paint brushes dipped in diluted solutions of various cleansing agents soon reveals the creamy translucent colour of the bone, but it must be born in mind that the original glue is waterbased and over zealous swabbing of the decks will lead to trouble. In addition water must be kept away from the rigging where there is a tendency for the already fragile threads to fray and almost to dissolve if wetted. Scraping with scalpels and chisels is often preferred, but this leaves a matt surface in place of the original slight polish.

The hull and those parts which have been removed from the model present no problem, but to clean thoroughly every surface of the masts and yards, the tops, caps and cross trees requires an absolutely methodical approach and total concentration to ensure that not one surface is left untouched and that, as far as possible, the existing rigging remains intact. This is the most difficult and tedious stage in the restoration. Most, if not all the masts and spars will be in position, wholly or partly rigged, so that all tools must

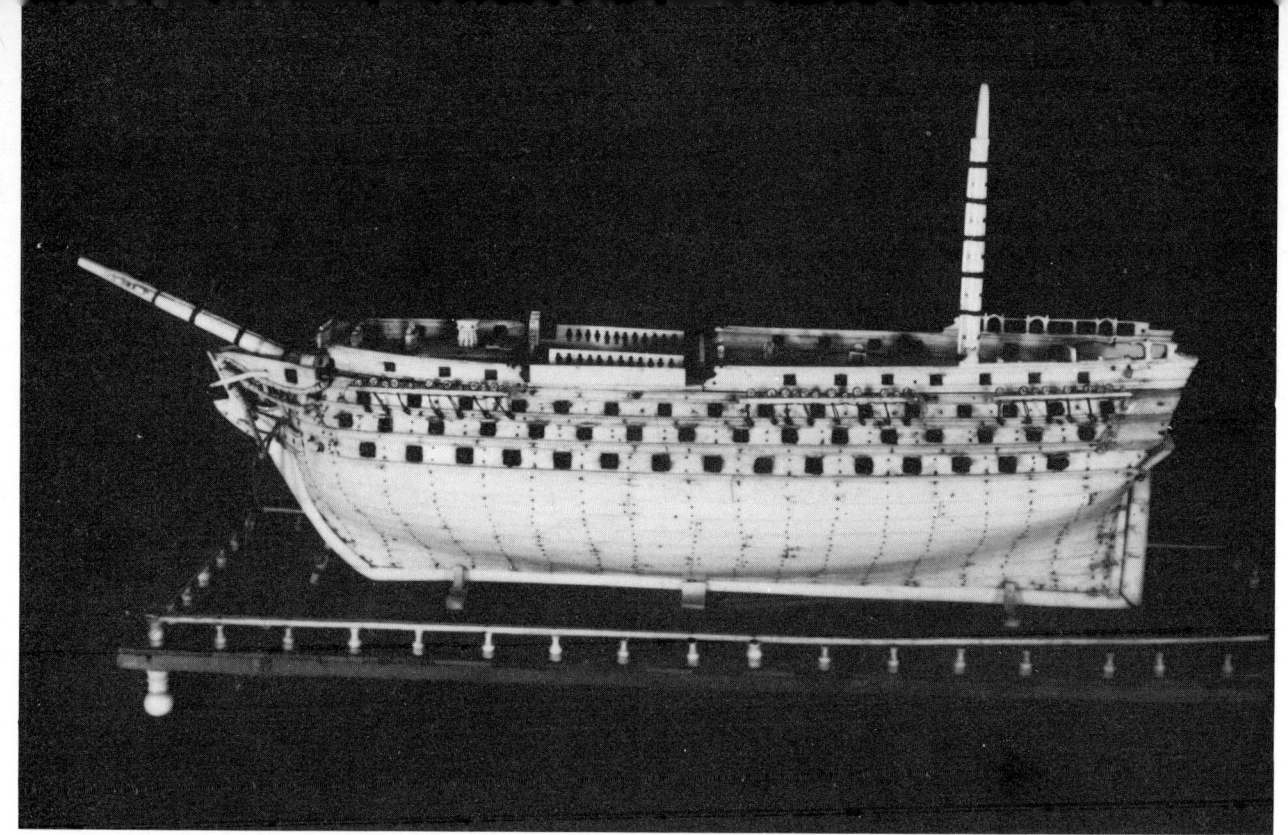

Above: A very good example of a model – in need of some restoration – of a French First Rate of the Napoleonic period.

be guided between the stays and braces – and since many are extremely sharp the danger of accidental damage to the rigging is acute. This is a painstaking and exacting task, requiring several days to complete.

Throughout the stripping and cleaning procedures the restorer is also 'getting to know' the model – and incidentally the original makers. For in order to restore with sympathy and discretion it is essential to have a detailed and dispassionate awareness of long-dead fellow craftsmen's work, to understand the style as well as the quality of the modelling. It follows therefore that the restorer should always be a better modeller than his predecessors and he must also be able to adapt and subordinate his

own style and standards to theirs.

Repair Due to the toughness of bone and the fact that most individual items on the models are carved from the solid, actual mending is a relatively minor operation. Masts and spars that have snapped cleanly can be securely and invisibly mended. The crosstrees, cut and filed in one piece, sometimes split along the grain of the bone and must be repaired *in situ* if necessary, and the peculiarly French decorative rails around the waist sometimes require attention, as do those figureheads having a raised arm peg-jointed at the shoulder. The splash boards and scrolling at the bows and the intricately fretted pieces making up the stern and quarter galleries are frequently loose and work in that area may also include some delicate repair of the gold foil or coloured paper window frames.

Replacement Retain all that you can, replace only what you must.

As a result of parts being either lost or broken beyond repair, replacement work obviously varies in extent from model to model. A

simple list will best show the range of work commonly encountered: Jibboom; upper masts and yards; mast trucks; stun'sail booms; crosstrees and mast caps; blocks; figureheads (parts of); anchors; guns, carriages and port lids; boats, gratings; ladders; rudder chains.

All parts are shaped from the solid using a hack saw and files followed by sanding, staining and polishing to match the parent model. Guns are turned or filed and if of brass can sometimes be adapted from those commercially available. In general lathe work is minimal and relatively crude.

Materials The acquisition of materials is not simple, but the restorer has the advantage that his requirements are small. Bone knitting needles and spatulas and oddments of ivory and brass are sought from junk shops, jumble sales and friends, and a diverse collection of aged timber is the result of collecting over a long period from a wide variety of sources. A life-long 'magpie mentality' is essential – as is a considerable amount of storage space!

A 'technical spin-off' from restoration work has been the discovery of ivory as a modelling material for general use. It is extremely hard but can readily be sawn, filed, drilled and painted, and for strength at extremely small sizes it can only be compared with metal.

Re-assembly A pleasant task, as the model gradually regains its pristine appearance of nearly two hundred years ago. Araldite is used throughout due to the hardness of the materials and the need for absolute permanence under unknown conditions of transportation and display in the future.

All the deck structures and fittings are replaced first, with the exception of the most delicate pieces on miniatures which are better left until after the rigging is completed.

Work on the outer surfaces of the hull will usually include replacing new or loose pieces around the figurehead and transom, dummy barrels and port lids for lower deck guns, and it is often necessary to re-fix the channels securely.

If whole mast assemblies have been removed as described above they are now returned to their sockets in the deck, temporary guys holding them erect until the glue sets. Sometimes the bowsprit needs re-glueing in its socket, which in turn involves dismantling the bobstay, the guys and the gammoning, and if the jibboom has been repaired or replaced it is now run out through the bowsprit cap and lashed at the heel in the proper fashion. Re-rigging can then commence.

Re-rigging Once again the amount of work required varies enormously. At best, much of the standing rigging will be intact and the running rigging will only need minor replacements and adjustments, but at the opposite extreme there might be extensive damage to the stays, shrouds and ratlines and the running rigging might require almost complete renewal.

If a whole mast was removed during the stripping down process the lower shrouds and ratlines will be hanging loose as complete assemblies (as supplied in some present-day plastic kits) and new lanyards are threaded through their deadeyes and those of the preserved stays.

A problem frequently encountered at this stage is that over the years the 'ropes' have stretched to such an extent that they remain slack even when the lanyards are drawn tight. With the offending stay still attached to the model and so dried up and fragile that it will part without warning if strained unduly, removing the deadeye and raising the bight in such a way that the correction will later be undetectable is not impossible, but neither is it easy.

The rigging sequence follows normal practice and all knots and seizings are sealed with matt varnish — usually at the end of a day's work so that the unwanted ends can be trimmed off as a 'starter' the following morning. Lower deadeyes are often re-fitted to channels and tops for absolute security and if the original lanyards have been left untouched over-length shrouds and stays are invisibly shortened at the head — another tricky operation. Topmast and topgallant stays often perform their actual function and are adjusted to re-align the masts.

When renewing the rigging a major problem is to match the colour and texture of the original cordage with modern materials. Many a restoration is spoiled by crisp, jet black rigging which, however well executed, is obviously not contemporary with the model. Constant vigilance is needed when at haberdashery counters, chandlers and hardware stores in order to build up and maintain a large and varied stock of cords, strings, twines and threads of every conceivable weight and texture. Colours range from off-white through buffs and browns to black, exact matches for individual models being acheived by a dyeing process.

CONCLUSION

At last the restoration is complete and the model stands, looking its age, but gleaming and trim as it did nearly two centuries ago when the luckless prisoners parted with it.

But how does one make the work look old? How is a brass cannon turned last week made to blend invisibly with the originals? And how is the visual 'softness' of an old model retained and matched? In the medieval sense these are the 'mysteries' of the craft of restoration,

and if I have been vague or silent about certain procedures it is because these are not so much learned as acquired through years of trial and error and a prolonged and intimate contact with the work of craftsmen from another age.

For the restorer there remains the peculiar satisfaction of having given a new lease of life to the model, and it has become a habit to leave, somewhere on the ship, in such a position that it will never be seen by anyone but another restorer, a name and a date — to be discovered when and by whom?

BOOKS AND RESEARCH

First and foremost must come 'the real thing', and HMS *Victory* at Portsmouth enables one to absorb the scale and texture and overall 'feel' of an actual ship-of-the-line. Nowadays the welcome proliferation of sail training ships allows the modeller to see square riggers under way with an ease and frequency undreamed of a generation ago.

Prisoner-of-war models can be seen at many museums throughout the country including The National Maritime Museum at Greenwich, and the Museum of Transport at Glasgow, The Science Museum, South Kensington, at each of which the staff are willing sources of advice and information. The models are not uncommon in the better antique shops — particularly The Parker Gallery, Albermarle Street, London W1.

The definitive work on the subject is Ewart C Freeston's *Prisoner-of-War Shipmodels* (Nautical Publishing Co 1973) and in his historical novel *The Lively Lady* (John Lane & Bodley Head 1946) Kenneth Roberts graphically describes conditions in Dartmoor Prison during the American War of 1812-1814.

For technical information C Nepean Longridge's *Anatomy of Nelson's Ships* must head the list (Percival Marshall 1961), and for miniature work the example set by Donald McNarry is unparalleled (*Shipbuilding in Miniature*, Percival Marshall 1955). In addition one can now obtain reprints of the contemporary Falconer and Steele, and the works of Harold Underhill are virtually indispensable.

WONDER 1860
AN ITCHEN FERRY BOAT

by Alastair Brown

Now living in the Isle of Wight, schoolmaster Alastair Brown is well placed to pursue his interest in building working scale models of a very varied range of local coastal craft. He is particularly concerned with the problems of designing the mechanisms for sailing these models by radio control.

The Itchen ferry boats were a variety of small inshore craft built on the Itchen River, Southampton, during the last century. The average length of the hull was about twenty feet but with a long running bowsprit and lengthy main boom the length overall was considerably more. These boats were used for fishing in Southampton Water and the Solent, and having only a small cuddy forward for accommodation, were not equipped for being at sea for more than one day. The main characteristics of these boats are a deep hull, with a broad beam and tumble-home, giving a wine glass shaped section (Figure 1). The hull is decked back as far as the mast, or to a bulkhead just abaft the mast. From there side decks continue to a point about four feet from the stern at which there is a second bulkhead forming the back of the cockpit and the front of a net compartment. The hull is completely open aft to allow the fishing gear to be dropped on to the raised floor of the net box (Figure 2).

In some of the boats that still exist today the hulls have been redecked and the side decking and coaming have been continued aft to meet the short length of deck just forward of the transom. The *Wonder* is such a boat.

The boats were all rigged as cutters, without a topmast, but carrying a topsail. The shape of the topsail varied; in some cases, as the boat grew older, according to the shape of an available surplus sail from another vessel. Mr J W Holness, the present custodian of the *Wonder* suggests a jib-headed topsail is most

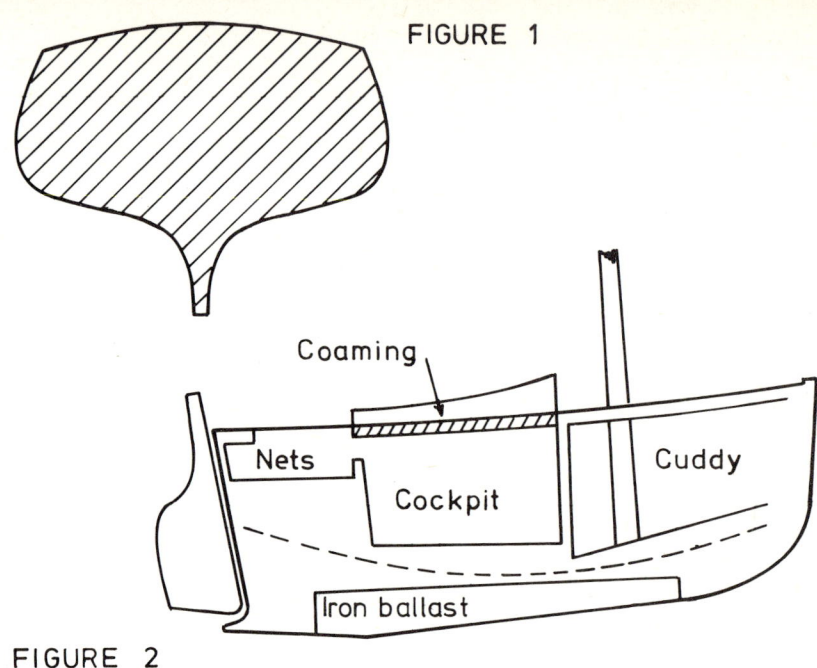

FIGURE 1

appropriate for that boat, whereas drawings of the *Nellie* show a distinctive jack-yard topsail. For my model I made one of each. The jib-headed topsail fits well, has a lower centre of pressure and, I suspect, is more efficient. From the model point of view the jack-yard topsail gives the boat a more interesting appearance. Either one can be accepted as authentic. The bowsprit is long, set slightly to port to clear the mast, but at an angle, so that when run out fully the tack of the jib is on the centre line of the boat. A staysail and jib are carried, both of moderate size, with halyards running to the hounds. The mast is stepped on the keelson, and supported by two shrouds and running back-stay each side, and a single forestay shackled to a short bumkin on the stem. The bowsprit is supported by a stay each side, and a bobstay, but no forestay, the jib being rigged flying.

During this century, the boats still working were fitted with inboard engines and had various fittings modernised. Rope lashing for the shrouds have been replaced by bottle-screws, and wire rigging used. The engine has since been removed from the *Wonder* and the boat has reverted to sail alone. Several of these trim little craft can still be found afloat. The *Wonder* is now kept on the Itchen by the Northern Bridge. At Woolston, in the shadow of the new Itchen Road Bridge, can be found the *Mermaid,* still in very much its original condition, like the *Wonder,* and another (whose name

FIGURE 2

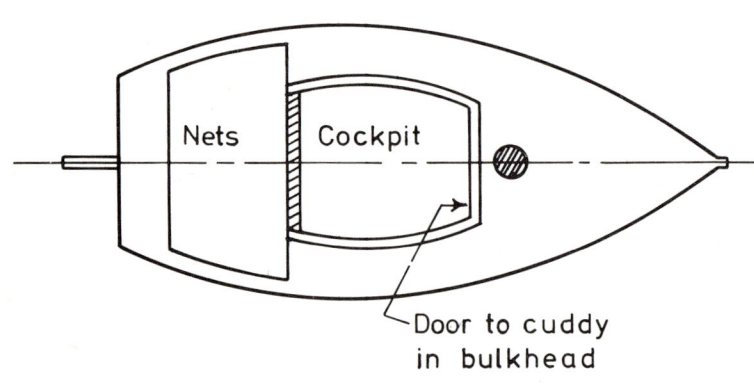

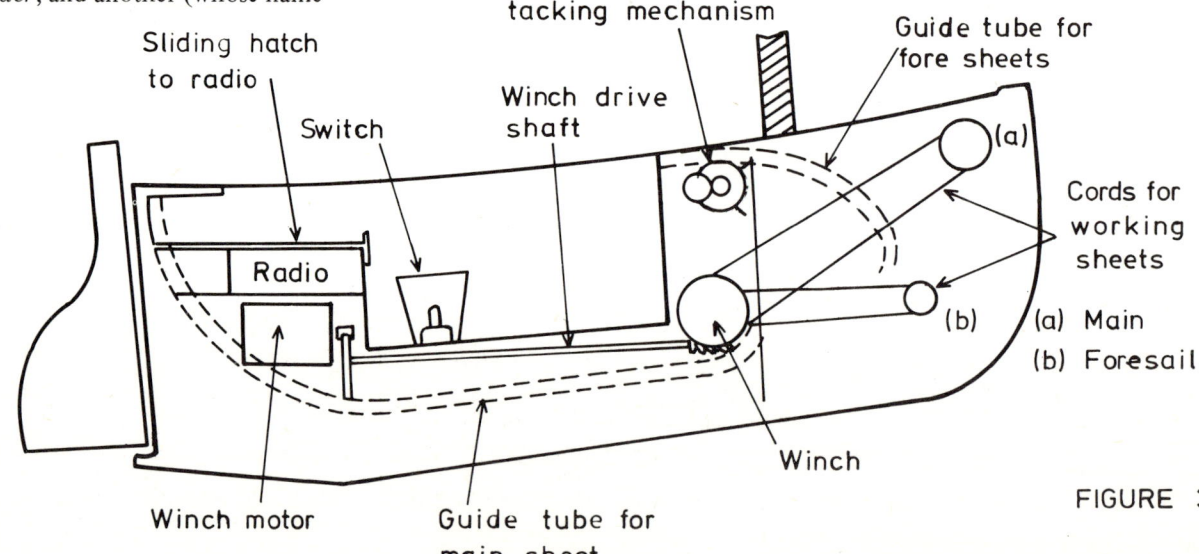

FIGURE 3

I did not discover) now with a cabin built over most of the cockpit and the mast mounted in a metal tabernacle. Even extensive modifications do not distract from the appearance of these boats, and the unknown craft looks a most charming yacht, which it would be a pleasure to own and sail.

I chose to build the *Wonder* as she is one of the two boats for which good drawings exist, the other being the *Nellie*. I am glad that I made that choice, as since starting work on the model I have been in touch with Mr Holness who did the drawings and who now looks after the boats, and received a lot of invaluable help from him. At his invitation I was able to go aboard the *Wonder* to settle those elusive details which always occur at some stage in construction of a model. He also took further measurements for me, and sent me new drawings containing additional details at my request. When beginning a model, it is certainly worth writing a few letters to museums, harbour authorities etc, as sometimes valuable information turns up. I was put in touch with Mr Holness by the Southampton Dock authorities, after I had written to them asking for details of ownership of several Itchen boats whose registration numbers I had found. Sometimes people who are unable to help directly can offer suggestions for other sources of information. I am gradually building up a file of replies for my own benefit. They may prove useful for future projects.

The *Wonder* was built at Northam in 1860 by Dan Hatcher, who built several such boats. Her hull is 19 ft long, 8 ft 3 in beam, with a draught of 3 ft 6 in. She was constructed from pine planks on oak frames. I decided to build a model to a scale of 1½ in to 1 ft (1/8) as that gives a hull length of 28½ in; a handy size, I thought, and just big enough to fit all the radio gear, batteries and other mechanics under the net compartment. That was the only place where I could make a removable hatch which would not show. I was able to fit the winch for the sails in the cuddy, just accessible through the cuddy door. Hiding full radio control in what is virtually an

open boat is quite a problem, and was a very tight fit in the end. There are literally yards of flex, rods and tubes competing with the lead ballast for room under the cockpit floor. A dirty rag in a galvanised bucket covers one electrical switch, and a wooden fish box containing a catch of three (real) crabs disguises a second one. The layout of the equipment is shown in Figure 3. The sheets are worked by continuous loops of cord taken from the winch round pulleys in the bows. I have

built the model showing the boat as she may well have been in the 1920s. This allows one to use the full sails of the original rig, and yet use more modern metal fittings where convenient. As the mast has to be removable (the model being 5 ft high) I wanted to use bottle screws for ease of dismantling the shrouds. They also allow me to use one shroud as a radio aerial, as the signal can pass through the screw.

The construction of the hull was plank on frame, using spruce for the

frames and deal for the planks. The reason for that choice was because a certain amount of clear varnish is used on the inside of the cockpit and I decided those woods would have an appearance in keeping with that of the original boat. Figure 4 shows the mid-ship section. The spars are from ramin. This is a good straight and close grained wood, tough enough for the job. Its colour was too light in comparison with the pine used on the full-sized vessel which has warm red-brown colour through the varnish. To alter the colour I used one coat of cedar-stained polyurethane varnish on each of the spars as a first coat. This stain was quite thin and was further subdued by sanding off most of that coat, just leaving it in the grain. Subsequent coats were clear varnish, and the final effect is good. Normally I would shudder at the thought of wood dye, but this treatment, using the stain very sparingly, has been completely satisfactory. The hull was finished with several coats of gloss black paint, rubbed down between coats. The main object of the gloss paint

is to keep the water out of the wood. When a satisfactory covering had been obtained I put a coat of semi-matt clear varnish on the topsides, which toned the gloss down to a used, dull appearance. The hull below the waterline was given a coat of dirty matt green to give the effect of the copper-based antifouling preparation of the original. The inside of the cockpit was painted in clear varnish and white, also toned down with semi-matt varnish finally. The floor boards were coated in a very dirty matt varnish which makes them look suitably grubby and 'walked on'.

Being a small open boat most of the detail is in the structure of the hull and the rigging. I have added a pair of oars and an anchor as essential gear. Inside the cockpit there is a bucket, fish box, the supporting legs, bolted on when the boat is moored, and a gaff hook (to help with congers, tope, and other large catches!).

The model sails well, with no false keel or rudder, and all ballast is internal, part of it moulded to fit in

the keel as did the iron ballast of the original. Care has to be taken to ensure the boat does not heel over too far, as not only is this uncharacteristic of this type of boat, but the model stands a good chance of being swamped if it is over for too long. As all the running rigging works, I am able to set sails to suit the wind by leaving the topsail off, and reefing the main and foresail as necessary.

Incidently, to those potential model shipwrights who are postponing the building of a model until they have a suitable workshop let me say I was able to construct this model in a small flat. My workbench was a board on the settee in the lounge for the most part. Naturally one requires a particularly understanding and patient wife if the model is to be successfully completed, but good work is certainly possible under such simple conditions. Improvisation and ingenuity can make up for lack of facilities, so few should be deterred from following this hobby if they have the inclination and the necessary skills.

I obtained much information about the Itchen ferry boats from *Inshore Craft of Britain in the Days of Sail and Oar*. Vol 2 by Edgar J March and *Sailing Craft of the British Isles* by Roger Finch. The latter book, incidentally, is an excellent source of basic information about most of the small craft seen around Britain during the last century. The general arrangement drawings, lines and sail plan are available from the National Maritime Museum, Greenwich, or the Science Museum, London. The model is now in the Southampton Maritime Museum.

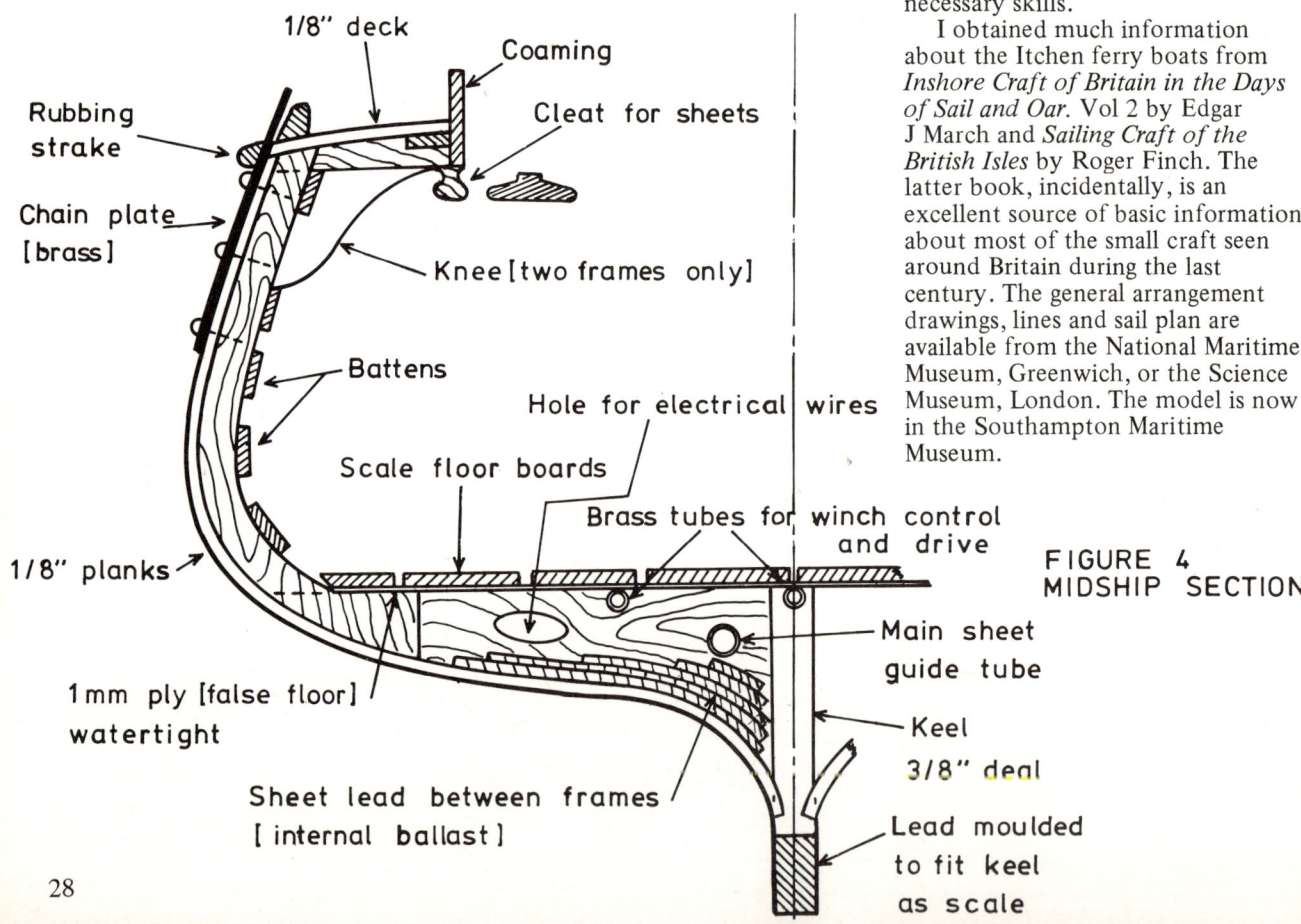

1/8" deck

Coaming

Cleat for sheets

Rubbing strake

Chain plate [brass]

Knee [two frames only]

Battens

Hole for electrical wires

Scale floor boards

Brass tubes for winch control and drive

FIGURE 4
MIDSHIP SECTION

1/8" planks

Main sheet guide tube

1mm ply [false floor] watertight

Keel 3/8" deal

Sheet lead between frames [internal ballast]

Lead moulded to fit keel as scale

THE GENOESE
LEUDO

by G Morino

Signor Morino lives in Sestri Levante on the shores of the Gulf of Genoa. He has a great interest in small sailing craft, and has spent much time researching local small craft and recording as many details as possible of these vanishing or vanished craft.

A group of *Leudi* pulled up on the shore at Sestri Levante in 1925. Note that they are always beached stern first.

All photos from the author's collection

During the nineteenth century a great number of small lateen-rigged vessels were built in and around the Mediterranean area, their design said to have originated with a ship called a *Liuto* or *Lembo*. In the Gulf of Genoa the particular local development was called a *Leudo*. Whereas the former was rigged with two well raked masts, each carrying a lateen sail, in the latter the elimination of the foremast and its replacement with a bowsprit and jib, coupled with a much increased forward rake to the mainmast created the *Leudo*.

In his *Etnologia Navale Ligure* C de Negri considers that the *Leudo* was derived from a small Spanish vessel called a *Catalano* or *Rivano*. There is no documentary evidence to support this theory, which is based on the supposition that the arrival of such vessels on the Ligurian coast must have been the logical consequence of Spanish influence in the Finale county. In those days, even as it is today, the Finale coast was devoid of harbours, and so any coastwise trade could only be carried on in small vessels. It was for this reason, it is thought, that the

Catalano was introduced from Spain in the seventeenth century. There is a painting by Ferdinando Glacer in 1629 purporting to show *Catalani* lying on the Finale Marina shore in 1600, which would appear to offer some confirmation of this theory.

Today the *Leudi,* those typical boats of the eastern part of the Gulf of Genoa, are virtually no more, for their traditional cargoes — sand, cheese, wine — are either no longer required or are transported by other and more economical means. At the time of writing I know of only six. There are two in Riva Trigoso, both of which have been stripped right down, while nearby is the recently

restored *Nuovo Aiuto di Dio (New God's Help)*. In Sestri Levante is one which has been 'ruined' by having the mast set plump upright and fitted with a form of spanker. The remaining two are in Santa Margherita Ligure.

It is a regrettable fact that craft which we know as *Leudo* were more often than not listed in the Italian Register as *Tartane* or *Bilancella*. The only reference I have found to *Leudo* as such was in some official statistics of 1867, where three vessels were entered as *Leudo*. However it is well known that a great number of these boats were built. In the county of Sestri Levante and Riva Trigoso alone there were at one time well over a hundred.

One of the last of these vessels to be built, though again registered as a *Bilancella,* was the *Due Fratelli Castagnola* (the *Two Brothers Castagnola*) ex *San Paolo*, launched at Lavagna in 1913. This vessel was 15.19 m in length from the foreside of the top of the stem to the after side of the sternpost, 4.43 m breadth to the outside of the planking, and 1.56 m deep internally from top of keel to deck beam. She is still in being today, but stripped right down — a condition which made lifting the details for the preparation of my plans very difficult. Nevertheless I am satisfied that they are truly representative of one of these vessels.

My researches have revealed that there were three different types of *Leudo,* each designed for a particular traffic. The first had a large hull, but with a low deckline, and was used to bring in sand lifted from the mouths of rivers in the Ligurian and Tuscany coasts for building houses. In fact it is claimed that most of Rapallo and Santa Margherita Ligure were built with sand brought in by the *Leudi*. My plans are for one of these vessels.

The second and third types both had a much higher deckline and were used for the transport of wine and cheese. The wine carriers brought their cargo from Elba to the Ligurian coast, and from Sardinia to the Gulf of Genoa, in large barrels stowed below and on deck. These were often

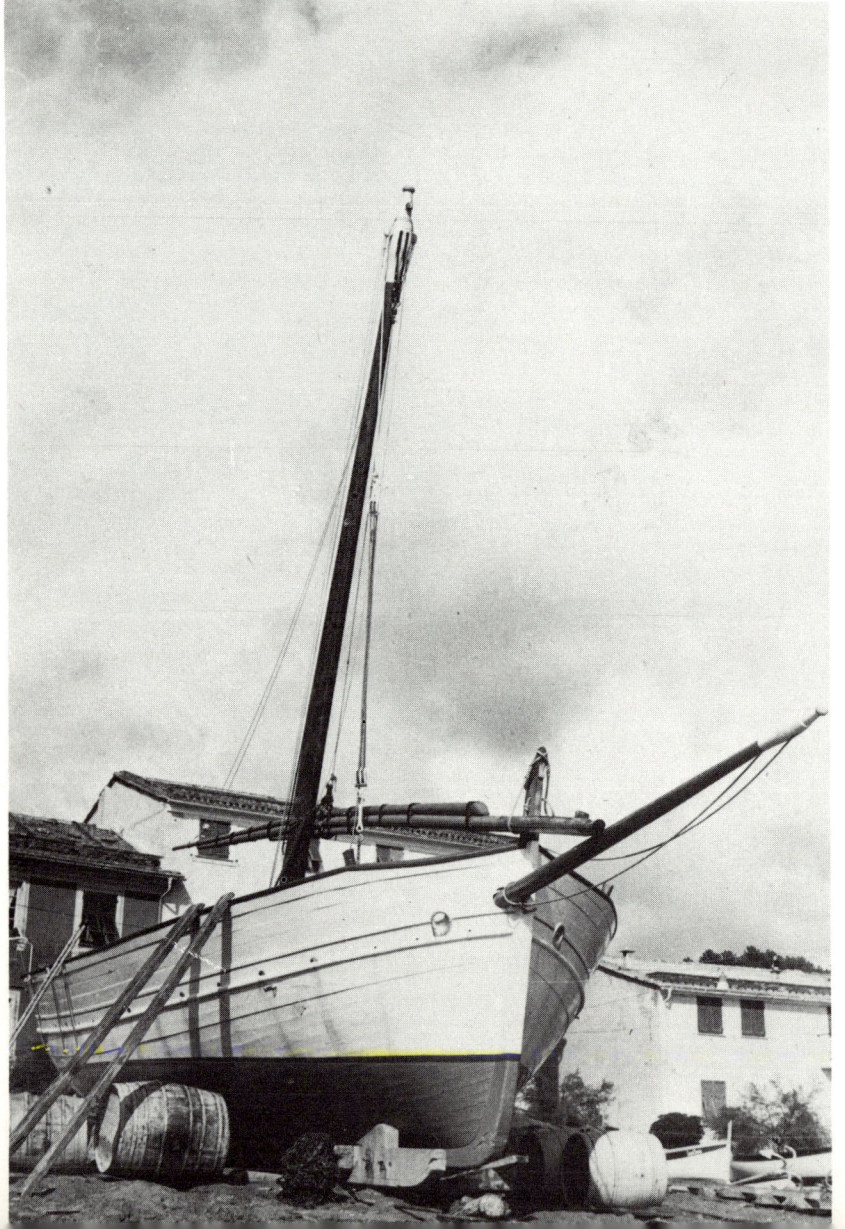

A wine type *Leudo*. Note the 'swelling' at the top of the mast for the sheaves, and the built yard.

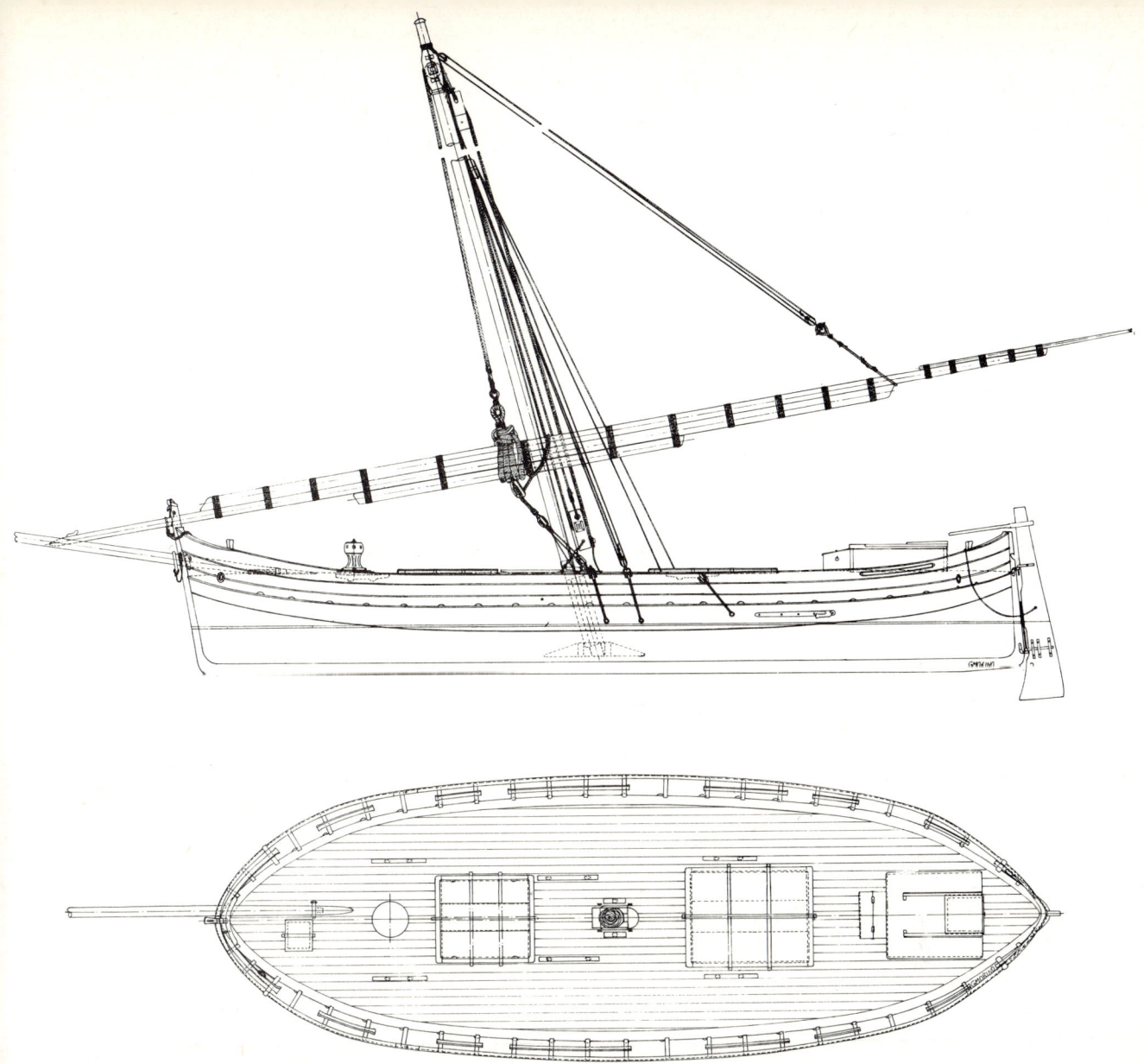

landed by being put over the side into the water when the boat grounded in the shallows off the shore, when they were hauled ashore with the aid of long ropes.

The cheese carriers were the mainstay of the families living on the Ligurian coast. They traded from Sardinia to Liguria, Piemonte and Lombardy, returning with such cargoes as firearms from Brescia, cloths and agricultural implements from Piemonte, and hand made goods from Liguria.

During the Second World War several of these craft were fitted with oil engines, which gave them a speed of 6 to 7 knots. They were used by the German forces as ammunition supply boats and as ferries along the Ligurian coast.

Recently I had the good fortune to meet in Riva Trigoso an old sailor who had worked in the *Leudi*. Among his reminiscences was the following.

'My earliest memories are of the sand. I was ten years old at the time, and we were continually going out in the boats to steal sand. Licences were difficult to obtain from the authorities, and as the shore and the river mouths were desmenial land, the Customs guards were very vigilant and strict. We were allowed to take on board sand from the mouth of the river Magra every two or three months, but only after we had obtained a permit for a 'draw' of sand from the mouth of the river. The usual way of loading the sand was in baskets carried on the shoulder, bringing it up a plank laid between the shore and the deck. If we sighted the Customs guards then we took flight very quickly. With all this thieving going on, before long the shores became devastated, and

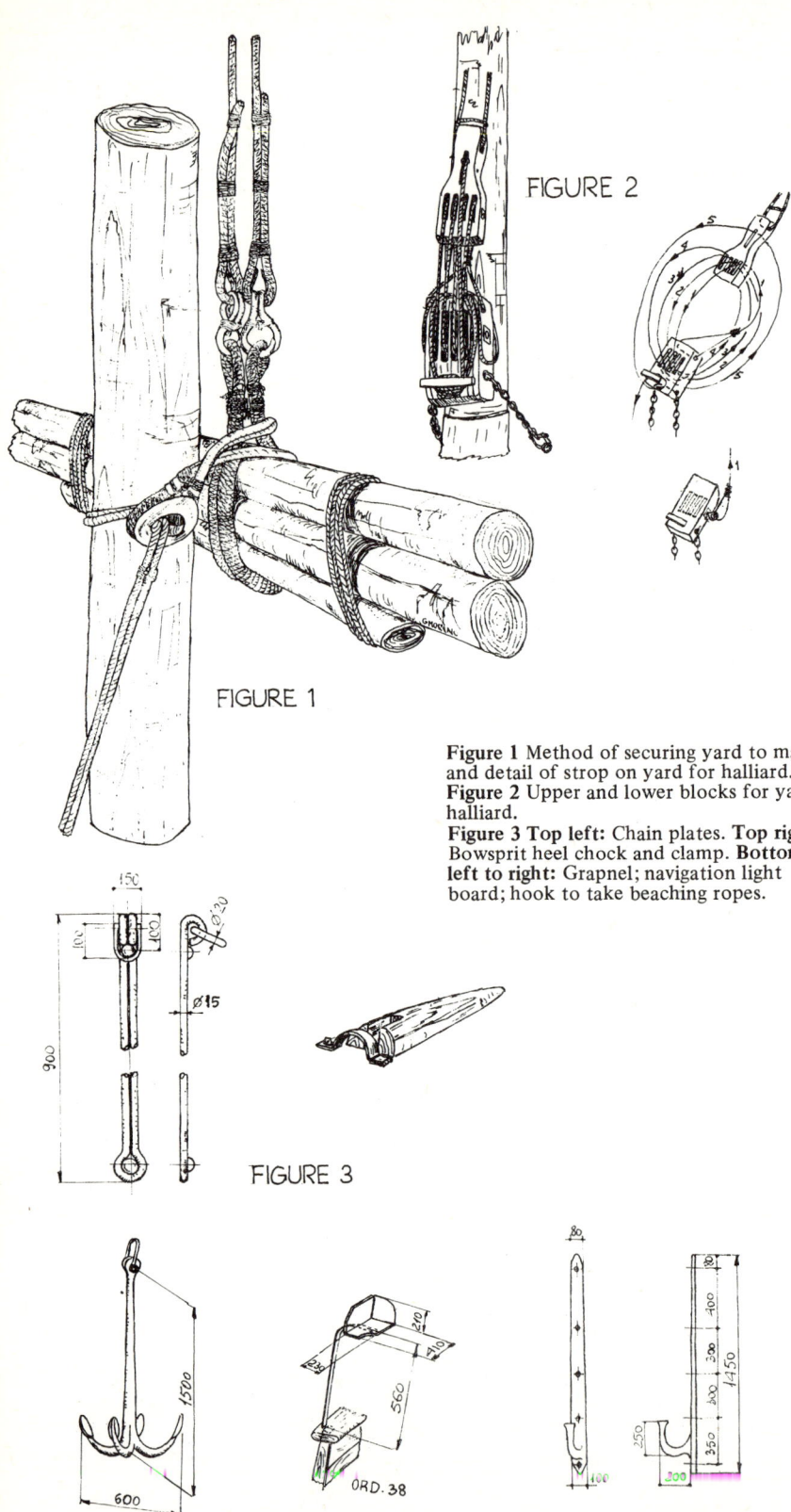

FIGURE 2

FIGURE 1

Figure 1 Method of securing yard to mast, and detail of strop on yard for halliard.
Figure 2 Upper and lower blocks for yard halliard.
Figure 3 Top left: Chain plates. **Top right:** Bowsprit heel chock and clamp. **Bottom left to right:** Grapnel; navigation light board; hook to take beaching ropes.

FIGURE 3

so the Customs guards became more vigilant than ever. So then the *Leudi* began to transport wine from Gallipoli (a town on the heel of Italy south of Taranto), Elba, Sicily and Pantellaria. We used to make two or three trips each year from August to October, each lasting between seven and fifteen days, and we used to be paid between eight and ten lira, depending on our ability. From Sardinia we carried vegetable oil, wine, cereals, almonds, cheeses and hand made goods. From Liguria dried chestnuts and slates.'

THE FRATELLI CASTAGNOLA

The bow is of the Catalan type, with the stem carried well above the top of the bulwark and having its top cut off at an acute angle and shaped like a cleat. The keel is of the usual type with keelson and false keelson. The floors are notched over the keel; the frames are bolted to the floors and end below the deck waterway. This is pierced with square holes through which pass the bulwark timbers to be bolted to the head of each frame. There is the usual clamp below the deck beams. A ceiling is laid on top of the floors to the turn of the bilge, and there is a cargo batten on the turn of the bilge. There are twenty strakes of planking on the hull on each side up to deck level.

The mast is of the lateen type, well raked forward, octagonal at the bottom, with the heel tenon fitting into a strong step. Where it passes through the deck and lies against a beam it is protected by being wrapped in leather at this point. The opening in the deck is covered with waterproofed canvas well secured with nails. At the head of the mast two sheaves are fitted, with a cheek piece each side to take the sheave pin. The mast was supported by two single tackles, both fitted on the side away from the yard, and leading to the second and third chain plates outside the bulwarks.

The lateen yard is of the built type, the parts being held together with lashings. At the forward (lower) end it is finished off in a curious hook shape to take the tack of the sail. Immediately above this point there is a heavy cleat to take the strop of the tackle controlling the end of the yard. When lowered the yard is lashed to the stem by a line passing through a hole in the stem, round the yard and back to that cleat on the top of the stem.

The yard is held to the mast by a heavy strop. A thimble was seized in a bight at the centre of the strop, the two free ends passed round the yard and the mast and brought through the thimble and led down to and made fast to the upper block of a tackle used to haul the whole assembly tight once the yard was in place. The lower block of this tackle was shackled to the eye of the forward chain plate on the bulwark, with the halliard end being made fast to an adjacent cleat.

The yard was raised and lowered by means of a heavy tackle. A single strop with a thimble eye at each end was passed twice round the yard, finishing with both ends above the yard. One end of a heavy rope was seized to one eye of this strop, and the free end was taken over one of the two masthead sheaves, down to and through the hole at the top

of a heavy fiddle block, back over the second of the masthead sheaves to the other eye of the yard strop, to which it was seized. This fiddle block had four sheaves in its lower part, with a single sheave in the neck above these. Secured by a strong chain to the base of the mast, on its after side, was a rectangular four-sheave block, with a cleat on the after face below the sheaves. The halliard was passed through a hole at the top of this lower block, up to and through the series of four sheaves in the two blocks; on leaving the last sheave in the lower block it went up to and over the single sheave in the neck of the fiddle block and down to the cleat on the face of

Below: Much detail can be found in this deck scene of one of the barrels being put overside. Particularly clear are the upper and lower blocks for the yard halliard, and the construction of the yard. It is interesting to note that the halliard has been disconnected from the yard strop, otherwise with the yard lowered the two blocks could not be in this position.

the lower block. The upper end of the yard was steadied by vangs passing through the eyes of a single strop fitted to the yard about one fifth of its length from the peak.

The lateen sail was bent to the yard with seizings passing through cringles in the bolt rope. There were reef bands on the sail. The jib, because of its enormous size in comparison to a normal one, was often called a spinnaker. In their early days some *Leudi* carried a large square sail, referred to as a course, which was substituted for the lateen sail when the wind was a fresh breeze. This type of *Leudo* was called a *Latine* and used mainly for fishing, when it did not hoist the jib.

On deck the *Leudo* had all the fittings usually associated with a small sailing vessel — bitts, cleats, navigation lights, anchor (grapnel), hand winch, capstan, two large sweeps, etc. The small boat was always towed astern, except in heavy weather. The wine type vessels carried ten barrels of 600 litres

A wine type *Leudo* being brought ashore. Note that the upper block of the yard halliard is at the top of the mast when the yard is in the lowered position. The horizontal black line on the white of the hull between the deck scupper holes and the waterline, to the right of the second figure from the left, is the heavy hook piece fitted permanently on the outside of the hull (each side) to take the ropes used for hauling the vessel ashore.

capacity on deck, with a further twenty of 2400 litres capacity stowed below deck in the hold. The crew consisted of a sailing master, boatswain and two sailors. The master and bosun shared watches, each with one sailor, on the usual four hours on and four hours off basis.

PLANS

The full set of plans for the *Fratelli Castagnola* prepared by the author comprise:- sheet 1, lines and body plan; sheet 2, profile with yard lowered; sheet 3, rig; sheet 4, deck plan; sheet 5, isometric constructional

section; sheet 6, details of yard trusses; sheet 7, detail of halliard blocks; sheet 8, sundry fittings; sheet 9, detail of masthead sheaves; sheet 10, detail of bowsprit sheave and lower end of yard.

Nos 1 to 5 are drawn to a scale of 1/33.3 whilst Nos 6 to 10 are on sheets size 290 mm x 180 mm.

All enquiries about the purchase of copies of these plans, and of these and other photographs of *Leudi,* should be made to:- G Morino, c/o Cas Post, Via A.Romana, Occ Le 169/9, I 16039, Sestri Levante, Genoa, Italy.

'Europa'

by P N Thomas

Some time ago the editor commented on the variety of requests which he had received regarding material for *Model Shipwright*. One of the items mentioned was cargo vessels of the post-war period. Shortly afterwards one of our local modellers asked if I had anything in the way of a modern single hatch coaster, so I had a look around and came across the vessel which is the subject of the plan.

The last thirty years have seen a great change in the shape of ships. The coaster to which we were accustomed was 'shipshape', with a gently raking stem and a small amount of flare, one or two pole masts with derricks, and a single funnel aft of a low superstructure. The line of the bulwarks swept aft in an attractive sheer. The changes in appearance have been gradual and we have grown used to each feature as it altered, with the result that the present day coaster does not shock us. Try to imagine how you would have felt if you had been cut off from ships for thirty years and suddenly saw for the first time a modern coasting vessel. The bow raked heavily forward with an exaggerated flare, fine lines forward with a knife sharp bow, no sheer at all and with all lines running horizontal. The bridge is piled high at the stern and the masts are in the form of bipods, tripods, goalposts or a mixture of these. Throw in with all that a bulbous bow and your agony would be complete. Yet these coasters have an attractive appearance – quite rakish in fact, as demonstrated by the drawing.

Unseen improvements which have

FIGURE 4

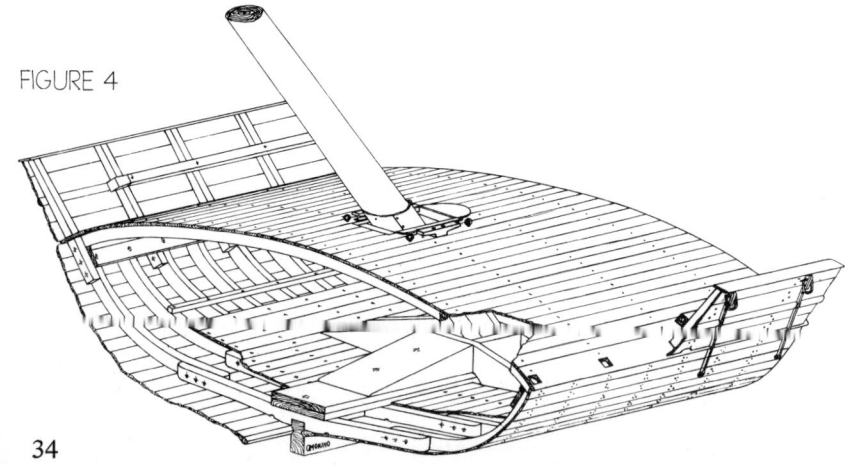

type Motor Coaster

been incorporated are the steel hatch covers and the hydraulic deck machinery. No longer the laborious business of hammering out wedges, removing steel battens, lifting out heavy hatch boards and finally the steel 'H' beams across the hatch opening. Now the crewman hitches a tackle on to an eyeplate on the steel cover and the winch hauls the self stacking sections clear of the hatchway in a matter of minutes. With modern deck machinery gone are the days when the winch driver stood behind a noisy clattering steam winch peering through clouds of vapour, pushing and pulling heavy levers. Now he stands on a perch

high above the deck with two small pedestals in front of him, each carrying little handles which control the hydraulic winches on the deck below.

A feature of the prototype which is slightly unusual is the bulbous bow normally associated with vessels three times her length — it was partly this that made me pick her as my subject. The bulbous bow is not really a new arrival on the shipping scene - some warships had them before the war. When the bulbous bow was developed after the war it was usually applied to large ships which were to be driven at high speed as it gave economies in fuel consumption. In

more recent years investigation has shown that even with small ships being driven at moderate speeds savings in fuel are possible when this type of bow is incorporated.

The prototype of the vessel shown on the plan was built by VEB Elbewerften in the German Democratic Republic especially for service between the North Sea and Baltic seaports, and was called the *Europa* standard type. The vessel was designed as a multi-purpose carrier and can handle such diverse cargoes as wood, grain, paper and even containers. Extensive use was made of models in test tanks in developing the hull form and the propeller.

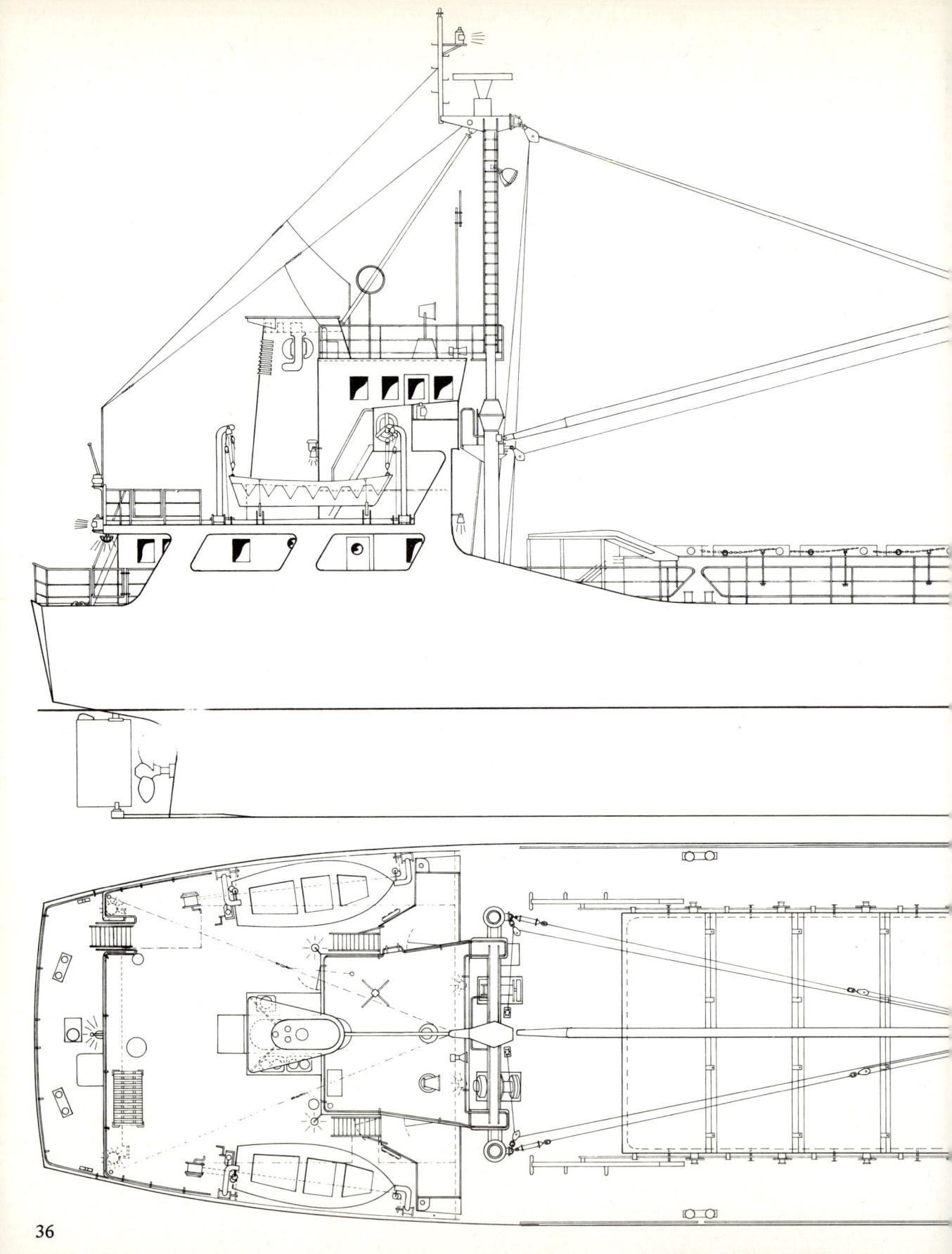

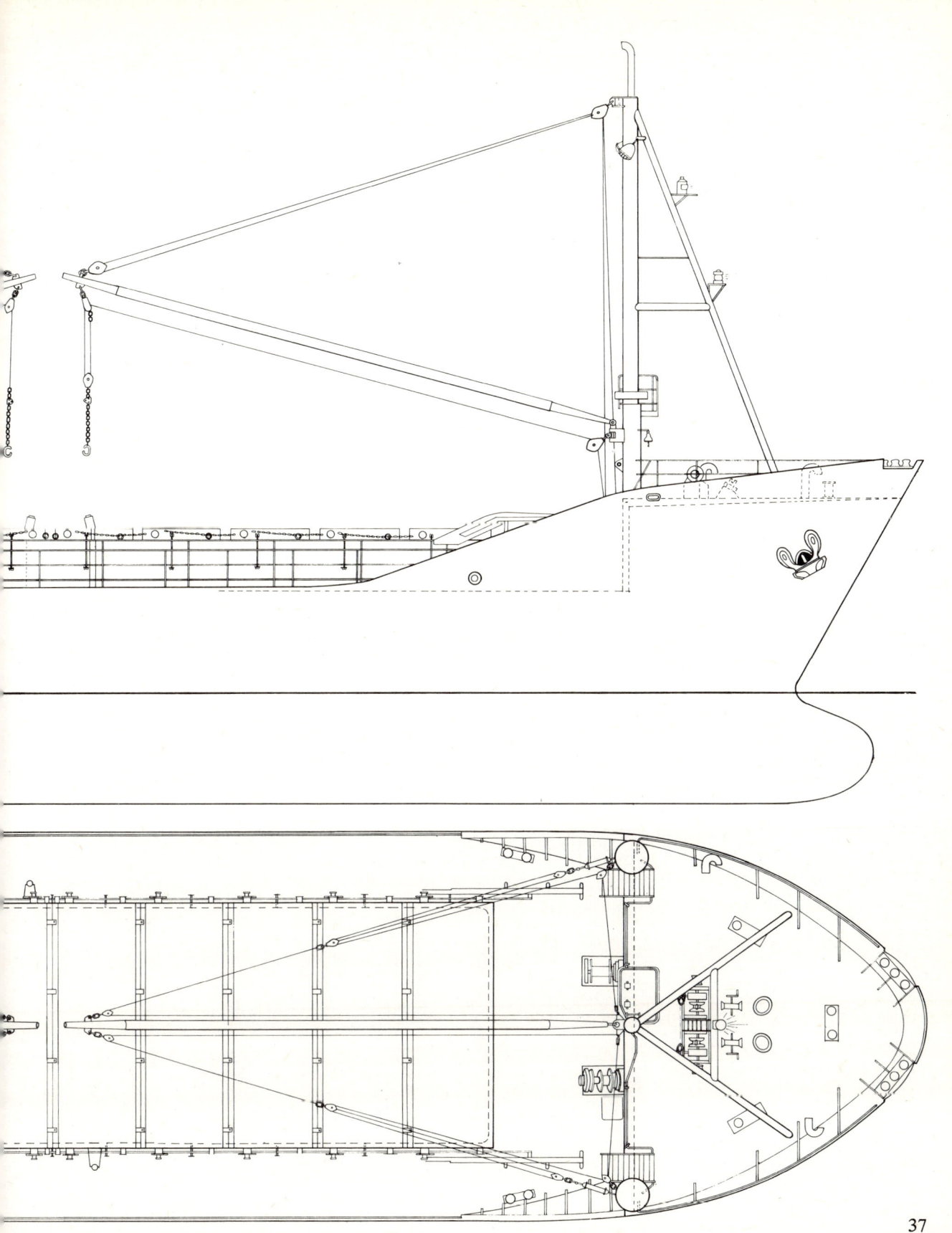

Most of the earlier vessels were built for the firm of Lars Rej Johansen of Oslo, hence the JO monogram on the funnnel, and all their names began Jo eg: *Joa, Jodur, Joett.* The ships have since changed hands and names, and most belong to two firms – Simonsen & Slang, Oslo, with names such as *Lys Blink,* and *Lys Sky;* and Per Haland of Egersund, who have given their ships such names as *Gullhav* and *Gullholm.*

The vessel is registered as 49.85 m x 10.10 m x 2.80 m draught with a gross tonnage of 199 tons. This is a surprisingly low figure for this size of ship but the deadweight tonnage (carrying capacity) is a more realistic 584 tons. The speed is quoted as 11 kts.

The plan is drawn to a scale of 1:50 giving a model 39 in long x 8 in beam. With a normal draught of 2¼ in the weight of the model will be 16 lb.

Despite the almost square midships section the block coefficient is kept down to 0.65 by the fine ends.

I have summarised the main colour details in view of the number of vessels involved. Generally speaking hulls would be light grey above water, with red or green boot topping; decks, red oxide, green or black. Hatch coamings often take the hull colour, deck machinery grey black, sometimes green. Masts and derricks white, cream or buff; boats, white or orange. Funnel in the owners standard colours. Superstructure almost always white.

I am indebted to the builders for permission to develop this plan from their original drawings, and for the photographs of the broadside launch and the *Briland.*

Paint colours for Lys-Line A/S Oslo vessels:-

Hull: Blue (International Paint Company's No 0802) on the hull amidships each side *Lys-Line* in white letters 4 ft high, bottom of letters sitting on the rubbing band. Ship's name on bow in white letters about 2 ft high.

Boot topping: Red (No 26).

Decks, hatches including coamings, covers and rails, winches, rails on cargo deck: Grey (No 0031).

Superstructure, masts, boats, rails aft and on bridge: White (No 26).

Funnel: White, emblem in hull blue.

Canvas covers to boats: Hull blue.

Below: A broadside launch of the modern single hatch coaster with typical bulbous bow.

THE LATEEN MIZZEN IN EUROPE

by Peter Hodges

Peter Hodges is perhaps best known for his articles on warships: he is for example the author of a book on 'Tribal' class destroyers, and is contributing the chapter on 'Guns and Gun Mountings' to the forthcoming Conway book 'Scale Model Warships'. He is also a modelmaker with a wide ranging interest in nautical research.

Comparatively little is known about naval architecture and even less of the precise rigging methods employed prior to the turn of the 16th century and models of ships of the Tudors and their European counterparts are often more conjectural than accurate. Contemporary engravings of 16th century shipping show a gradually improving appreciation of proportion and perspective, but nevertheless it is quite clear that the engravers (who were landsmen anyway) did not properly understand the function of much of the running rigging. Nor did they realise that the weatherdecks did not follow the sheer of the hull as it rose steeply towards the quarters and, in consequence, they show poop-decks sloping 'downhill' in an alarming manner which would have made them difficult to negotiate in harbour, let alone at sea.

So far as sails and rigging are concerned, an area that obviously confused these early engravers seems to have been passed on to modern artists and modelmakers. This is the manner in which the lateen mizzen was set and handled. In his interesting article on Portuguese caravels which was published some years ago in *Model Maker*, Manuel Leitao (whose name hints that he

was, perhaps, writing on a native subject) remarks 'A great deal of uncertainty exists regarding the actual handling of (these) rigs. First of all, there is doubt as to whether the lateen sails were hoisted inside or outside the lee rigging . . .'

Since I was about to embark on a miniature model of a four-masted 16th century caravel, and uncertain as to the correct leads of the lateen yards' rigging, I researched the subject at some depth to determine whether, in fact, the lateen sail should be set inside or outside its shrouds; and from that how, in practice, it could be transferred from side to side when the vessel went about.

Examination of a number of early engravings which appear in *The Macpherson Collection of Prints and Drawings* by M S Robinson, E Keble Chatterton's *Old Ship Prints,* and a study of Alan Villiers' *Voyage in a Kuwait Boom* in the *Mariner's Mirror,* Vol 48, Nos 2 & 4, indicated that there were two distinct forms of lateen mizzen, one belonging to Southern Europe and the other, and later, version belonging to Northern Europe. There were fundamental differences between the two styles which dictated how the sails were set and handled, and what was possible in this respect with one form, was impossible with the other.

SOUTHERN EUROPE

The lateen sail itself seems to have been born somewhere in the area of the Nile valley and Red Sea, and its use spread in the Middle Ages northwards and westwards across

the Mediterranean to the City States of Italy and along the southern coast of France. By the 15th century it was well established in the Iberian peninsula and had, indeed, spread northwards to our own native waters. Here it appeared as a mizzen and must have been of great value as a riding sail, while in Southern Europe it often remained as the principal sail supplemented — in the case of the caravel — by square sails on the foremast.

The caravel rig has sometimes been likened to the modern barquentine but the similarity is really only an accidental one. The barquentine was, in effect, the successive cut-down of the ship rig (via the barque), and *Cutty Sark* was so reduced in her final active days. The caravel, on the other hand, was a fore-and-aft rigged vessel with the addition of a square-rigged foremast, and more nearly the ancestor of the topsail schooner. The lateen of this period was directly copied from the Arabic sail and had two special characteristics. The first was that its mast was supported by shrouds terminating in tackles, rather than in deadeyes and lanyards; and the second was that the tie from the yard to its purchase led from forward through a sheave or sheaves, to the *after* side of the mast.

Let us now see how this sail was set and how it was handled. Figure 1 shows the mizzen of a typical Iberian ship of the mid 16th century. The wind is from somewhere forward of the port beam and the sail is sheeted home to a bumpkin. It is set 'outside' the lee shrouds, which serve no useful purpose and were, in fact, slackened off completely. They are shown set-up in Figure 1 only to demonstrate the relative position of the lateen yard. Note that the shrouds are secured inside the poop bulwarks and not to channels and that they have no ratlines; for although ratlines can be spread across shrouds from the higher deadeye upwards, they obviously cannot be attached to a moveable tackle. Further, the mizzen top at this time was diminutive and could hardly by counted as a 'fighting-top' while, in addition , there was little need to go aloft for sail-handling.

The lead of the tie dictates how the sail is transferred when the ship goes about, and the procedure is shown in Figures 1 to 4. In Figure 2 the sheet and the vangs have been paid out, and the yard has been hauled upright by the tackles (oddly called 'bowlines') attached to its foot. Notice that for this purpose, these bowlines lead sharply backwards towards the break of the poop. At this vertical, or near vertical, position the sheet is either cast off from the bumpkin or from the clew to allow the sail (which is only *loosely* confined to the yard) to be passed around in the direction of the arrow, rolling right over its yard. At this time, the new weather shrouds would

be set up by their tackles.

The next action is to haul the foot of the yard athwartships to starboard, while the peak crosses to port. Even though the new weather vang could be hauled in to steady the peak, it must have 'flopped' across with a frightful lurch. The sheet now has to be re-bent to the clew (or re-rove through its lead-block on the bumpkin) – Figure 3 – and finally the sail is sheeted home 'outside' the slackened lee shrouds. The fact that the yard, during the mid-point of its transfer, would lie almost like a topmast before the mizzen mast, precluded any type of top that projected forward and makes the presence of the typical Mediterranean 'bucket-style' top especially significant. This lateen was obviously a very flexible sail – provided one accepted the longwinded procedure necessary on going about. In Figure 5 (taken from the title page of a book printed in Barcelona in 1592) the same sail is set for running, when the vangs and bowlines act almost like square yard braces, and the clew is sheeted home amidships to the break of the poop. This is the position in which the sail was frequently found in the rudimentary 'galleons' once popular as drawing-room ornaments.

The set of the sail on either tack,

or for running, is easy to see; what is confusing perhaps, is its appearance when furled. Because the yard was physically 'outside' the shrouds, it could not be lowered to the deck in the fore-and-aft line unless the lee shrouds were cast off, and this is precisely what was done. The lower tackle block on each shroud was provided with a toggle-and-becket arrangement, so that when the tackles were eased, each shroud could be released. The yard was then lowered for a harbour stow, whereupon the unattached shrouds were passed *over* the yard and re-secured. The yard, with its furled sail, was then re-hoisted, (Figure 6) *but now inside the shrouds.* Alternatively, having initially lowered the yard, the lateen might be stowed in stops *and re-hoisted outside the shrouds,* ready to be set by a sharp haul on the sheet. It is often so shown in engravings of ships at anchor, but this in no way alters the fundamental features of the Iberian lateen mizzen.

Some aspects of the mizzen mast itself are worth noting. It was a mere stump compared with its main and fore partners, and had no fore-and-aft stay leading forward. This was because any such stay would have fouled the yard in its path around the forward face of the mast in going

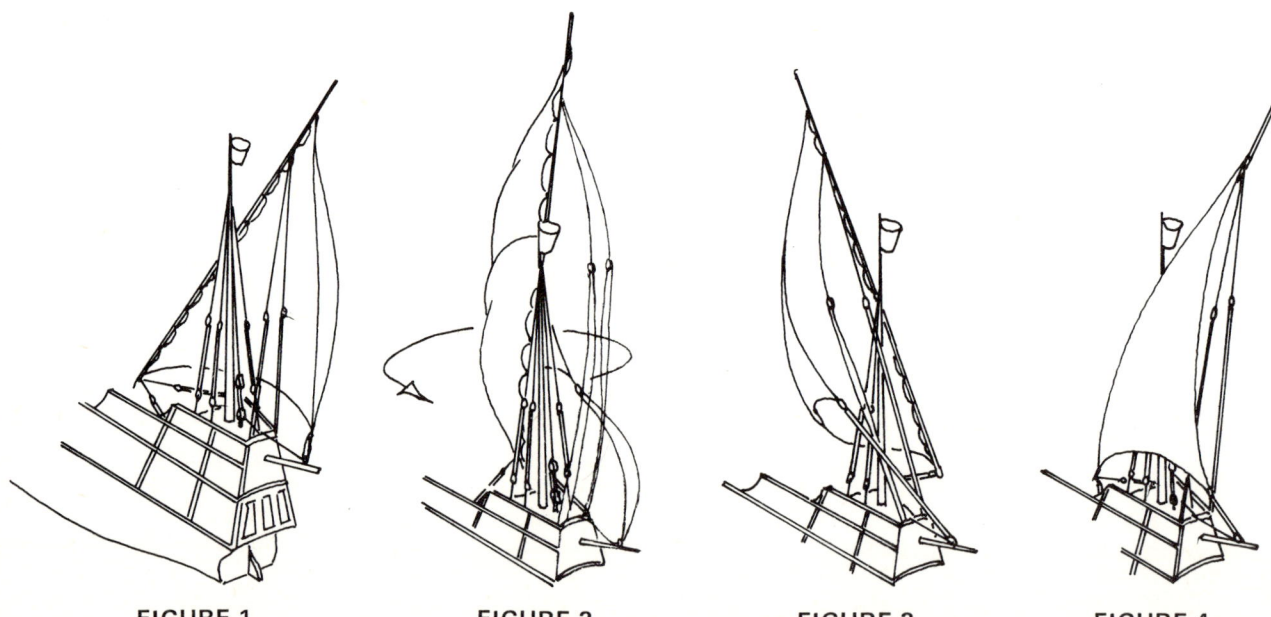

FIGURE 1   **FIGURE 2**   **FIGURE 3**   **FIGURE 4**

about. But not only did this movement preclude a mizzen stay; it also made the lead of the main topsail braces problematical. Again, this seems to have confused the artists. Figure 7 shows the manner in which the topsail yards are often depicted in contemporary engravings. The fore topsail bowlines lead forward to the fore topmast stay and its braces lead backwards to the main topmast stay. On the main topsail, however, while (one assumes) bowlines lead forward to the main topmast stay, no conventional braces are shown. Lines run from the main topsail yardarms downwards to the maintop and these, in my view, are probably the cast-off main topsail braces.

Clearly, whatever 'side' the furled lateen mizzen yard found itself, there would be only a 50% chance that it would be appropriately positioned for making sail. Thus, the main topmast braces could not be led back to a natural point on the mizzen masthead (there being no mizzen stay to which they might otherwise have been attached) until the position of the mizzen yard to port or starboard of its mast had been established. If this supposition is correct, it would mean that, in a seaway, the same 'casting-off' procedure would be necessary before

the lateen yard could be transferred.

Later engravings of Spanish ships give two auxiliary tackles to the lateen yard and Figure 8, which is taken from one of Theodore de Bry's works dated 1594 shows them; in addition, he shows a standing backstay leading to the bumpkin. One tackle leads from the masthead to the foot of the lateen yard, perhaps to take its downward thrust, while the other serves as a topping lift-cum-peak halyard, doubtless to assist the raising of the peak when going about. It is interesting to note that it leads below the top so as not to restrict the movement of mariners in the top itself. Again, these tackles would have presented complications in going about, for both would need to be cast off to allow for the transfer of the yard.

A new feature is revealed in Figure 9, taken from the latest clear engraving of the period that I have come across. The original *Off the coast of Florida* — is attributed to the de Bry family and is dated 1609. As well as the 'new' standing backstay leading to the bumpkin (indicating that in all probability the Spanish were still transferring their mizzen yard around the forward face of the mizzen mast) a topping lift, terminating in 'crowsfeet' at the peak, leads forward to the

maintopmast head. This lift had been a feature of English ships for some decades and it is tempting to think that the Spanish copied them, the easier to top-up their lateen yards.

This standing backstay and the diminutive stature of the Spanish mizzen mast compared with the contemporary mizzen-topmasted English ships leads me to believe that, at least until the turn of the 16th century, the Iberians persisted with the old form of lateen.

NORTHERN EUROPE
The earliest examples of lateen mizzens in our own waters indicate that, not unnaturally, they were rigged (and therefore handled) in the established manner. The Science Museum model of an English ship c1485 — in other words, at the very begining of the Tudor period — shows a vessel with the then newly introduced three-masted rig. She has a small lateen mizzen, set outside twin shrouds without deadeyes or channels; and its yard is even constructed from two spars fished together exactly in the Mediterranean fashion. A photograph of this model appears as Plate III in Part II of the Science Museum booklet on the history and development of sailing ships. Within a few decades, however, a distinct change had taken place.

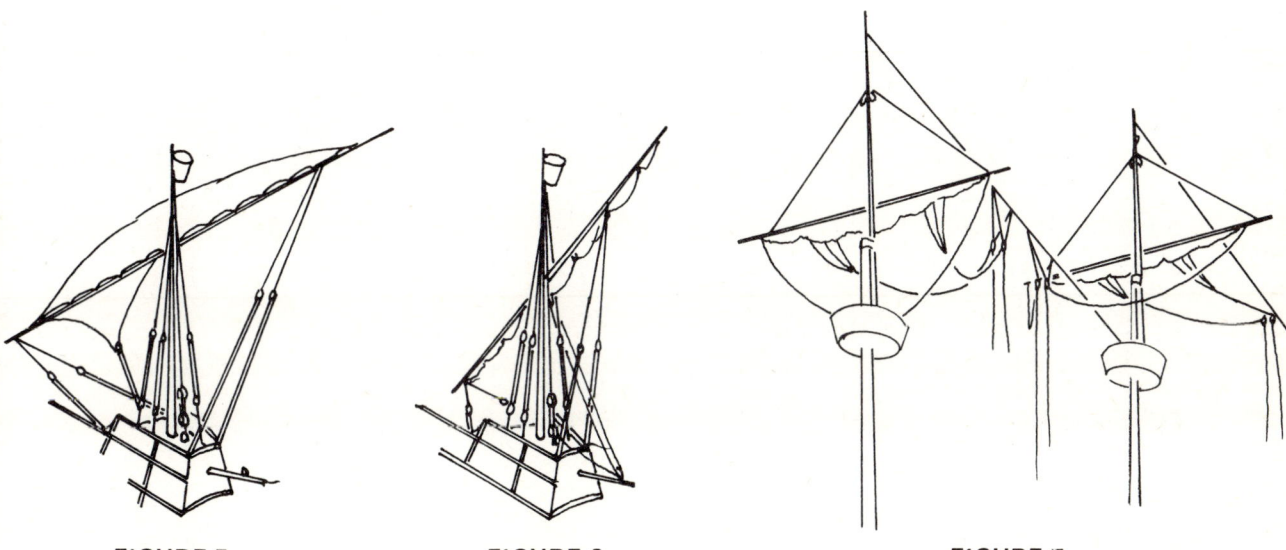

FIGURE 5   **FIGURE 6**   **FIGURE 7**

The mizzen shrouds (and those of the bonaventure, too, if fitted) were now set up by deadeyes and lanyards and were furnished with ratlines; while the mizzen top was circular like its fellows, and was much more of a 'fighting top' than its Iberian counterpart.

A flagstaff on the mizzen quickly grew into a mizzen topmast (noticably absent from Spanish ships), and a lateen 'topsail' on this mast is so frequently shown in engravings of the large Tudor ships that it certainly existed. Mizzen stays and mizzen topmast stays are also much in evidence, with main topmast backstays commonly leading to them. By no means the most ideal lead, perhaps, but eminently better than having no backstays at all. The same mizzen stays provided a transfer point for the topsail braces; and while the mizzen mast itself would have provided a stiffer point of contact (later, of course, adopted), the Elizabethans may have preferred to man their halyard falls on open decks between the masts, rather than at the mast-foot.

The very existence of a mizzen stay precluded the transfer of the lateen yard in the original manner; and further, unlike the 'calcet' masthead of the Mediterranean, the shrouds were laid over the trestle-trees, which themselves supported the cross-trees and top, with the sheave, or block, for the lateen tie positioned below it.

Imagine, then, the problems of setting this lateen yard so that its sail was outside the mizzen shrouds. The yard itself would need to be slung 'square yard fashion' in the first instance, with its tie, following Mediterranean practice, leading abaft the mizzen mast. This lead, together with the close proximity of the shrouds, would severely limit its movement towards the fore-and -aft plane, for unlike the lateen of Southern Europe, the shrouds could not easily be cast off. Further, when the yard was topped up to its characteristic angle, the yard would foul the top. Dropping it further below the top to alleviate this would inevitably mean that it fouled the diverging shrouds more quickly as it was 'braced' around: and, in short, the yard and sail would effectively be

little more than a triangular square sail – if the anachronism can be excused.

The crucial difference between this lateen and its forebears lay in the lead of the tie. This was reversed from the original and led from the yard through its sheave *forward* to a securing point *before* the mast, much as does the throat halyard of a gaff sail today. The yard was slung *inside* the standing shrouds and the sail was *set* inside them – a configuration which meant that it could not be transferred from side to side in the Arabic manner. Instead, the *foot* of the yard was 'dipped' around the lower after face of the mizzen mast – a procedure which will be familiar to all who have handled a dipping lugsail. Figures 10 to 12 show the progression.

Another important difference between the two styles of lateen mizzen was that the English utilised the 'bonnet' principle on their lateens as a means of shortening sail and, because it was easier to lace only canvas-to-canvas, the result was a lateen with a vertical 'knock' on the forward edge. Even when the

FIGURE 8

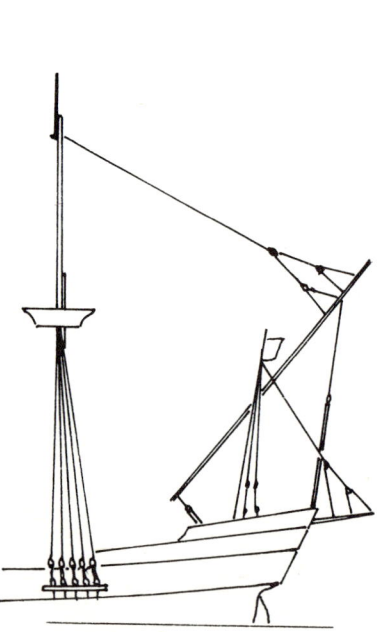

FIGURE 9

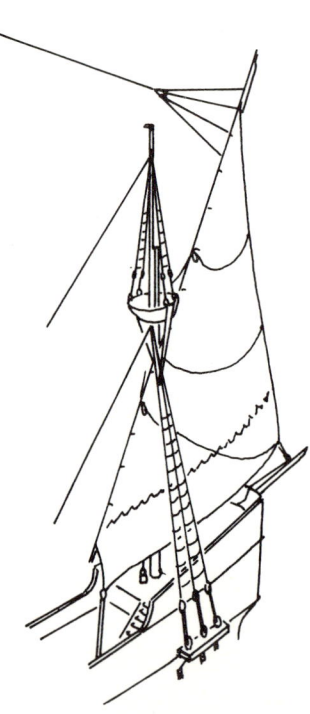

FIGURE 10

bonnet had been overtaken by reef points, the English lateen remained with a square knock, although, of course, it assumed a triangular shape with a reef tucked in. Obviously, because the lateen yard was out of balance in having the greater length abaft the mast, topping it up by bowlines was inefficient and thus a topping lift, often running from the main topmast or topgallant (and thus giving a considerable mechanical advantage) became a common feature. R C Anderson says in his *Seventeenth Century Rigging* that it is possible that these were, in fact, early forms of topmast backstay, but I am sure their purpose was solely to assist in bringing the lateen yard upright. It is hard to believe that the eminently practical Elizabethans would have chosen so flexible a support, which in any case would cease to exist while the lateen yard was being transferred.

Reverting for a moment to the lateen 'topsail', and having established how the Northern European sail was handled, the difficulty of transferring such a topsail yard in the Iberian manner can be imagined. On the other hand, by the 'dipping' process (aided by a topping lift to the topgallant masthead), it could be accomplished reasonably swiftly with, perhaps, two mariners aloft to guide the foot of the yard around the after face of the mast. In addition, there was no need to cast off the sheet to effect the transfer and this in itself was a great advantage.

Cumbersome as the lateen yard undoubtedly was, the handiness of the Northern European rig compared with the Southern is clear, and may be a clue to the oft-mentioned attribute of 16th century English mariners in their smart ship-handling.

When the change in lateen rigging took place is difficult to determine; and why it took place is a matter for conjecture. My own belief is that the Spanish and Portuguese, enjoying as they did an Atlantic seaboard, and venturing westwards and southwards towards the Americas and Africa, accepted the lateen as they found it, employing it more as a square sail (Figure 5) in the Trades, than as a fore-and-aft. The heavy standing backstay in the de Bry engraving mentioned earlier provides, one

might almost say, strong supporting evidence for this particular lateen function, and has its equivalent in the standing stay leading from the masthead to the counter in a modern yacht.

The English, on the other hand — and later the Dutch, freed from Spain — had the Channel and often a southwesterly to contend with as soon as they left harbour, and used the sail much more for its fore-and-aft attributes. In this respect, another engraving by the de Bry's is of particular importance. Dated 1601 and called *The Amsterdam attacked by East Indians*, it shows a Dutch ship with a 'northern' lateen mizzen, and maintopsail braces leading to the mizzen masthead. It makes an interesting comparison with *Off the Coast of Florida*, executed eight years later. Both styles of lateen needed a parral, which the early engravers were at pains to show (complete with enormous trucks) embracing the yard and the mast It would need to be slackened to transfer the yard and doubtless had a parral-tackle (as have present day Arab lateens); and although such

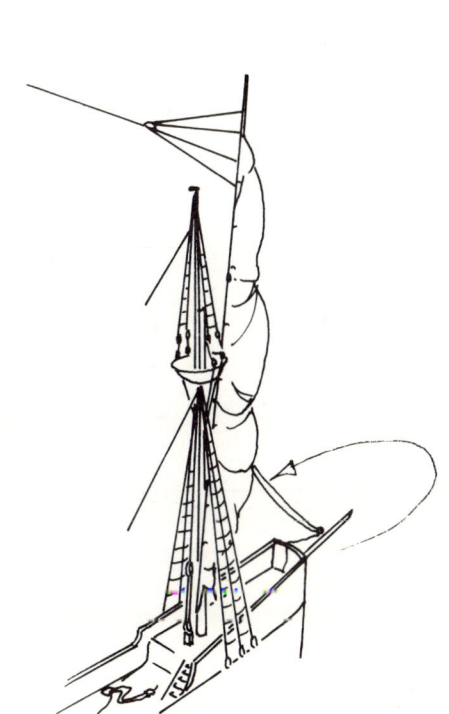

FIGURE 11

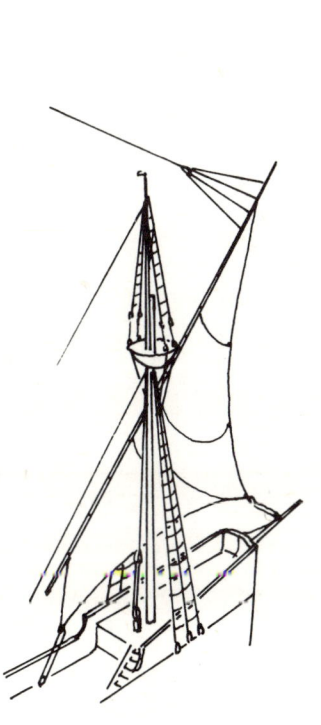

FIGURE 12

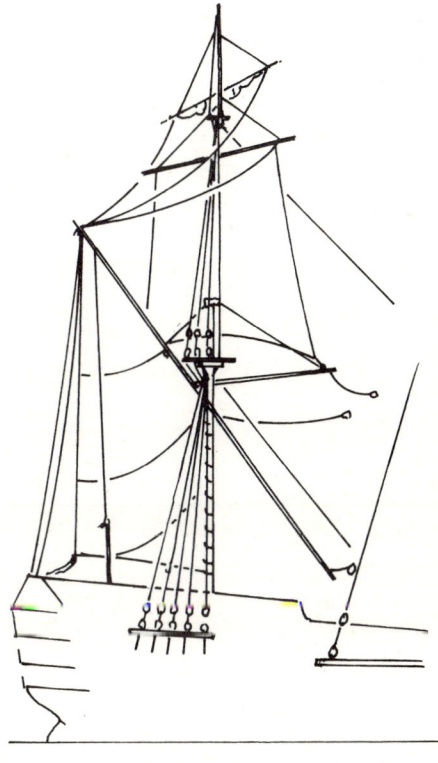

FIGURE 13

tackles are not shown in these 16th century works, their style is easily imagined.

LATER DEVELOPMENTS

The full lateen mizzen course continued to be set in English ships throughout the 17th century and into the 18th, by which time both the artists and the modellers of the day were producing highly accurate work upon which reliance may fairly be placed. In an engraving by Sartor after Thomas Baston of about 1720, the artists actually show the full lateen laid aback against the mizzen mast — a rarely portrayed occurrence. The sail would have chafed badly were it so set for long periods, but perhaps on short 'legs' to windward the sail was not transferred if, on going about, a long 'leg' was to follow, or the ship was soon to revert to the original tack.

A significant change to the mizzen mast generally in the 17th century came with the introduction of the square mizzen topsail. From diminutive beginings it gradually increased in size and was joined in due course by a mizzen topgallant and later still, a mizzen royal. Clearly these square sails provided all the fair wind requirements necessary, superseding this function of the mizzen course. Further, unlike the Iberian lateen which, as has been seen, could deliberately be set as a running sail, the northern equivalent was by a matter of geometry more constrained towards the fore-and-aft line.

From about the middle of the 18th century that part of the sail before the mizzen mast was dispensed with, and the vertical luff so created was laced to it. This produced a loose-footed sail similar to a gaff sail, but with a leach at a variety of angles to the vertical. It was still known as the mizzen course and was stowed by brails, that gathered it inwards and upwards towards the yard and mast.

Once this reduced version of the lateen had been adopted, there was no longer any need to transfer the yard when going about, although the complete yard itself was retained in the larger warships until the close of the 18th century. HMS *Victory* was built with a lateen yard which she retained for many years although, of course, she had a gaff-sail by the time of Trafalgar. It became customary to set the lateen yard to starboard of the mizzen mast, a practice followed by sprit-rigged vessels like the Thames barge, whose sprits are invariably to starboard.

The gaff-headed sail had been in existence elsewhere for a considerable time before it was finally adopted in all rates of British men-o' war, and various reasons why the half-barren lateen yard was retained for so long have been propounded. My own view is that it survived for a combination of all reasons. The forward part provided a counterpoise for the after; its length made it useful as a spare spar; constrained fairly rigidly by vangs and bowlines, the peak presented a usefully high point to which the upper mizzen yard braces could be led (Figure 13). Even when the lateen yard was succeeded by the

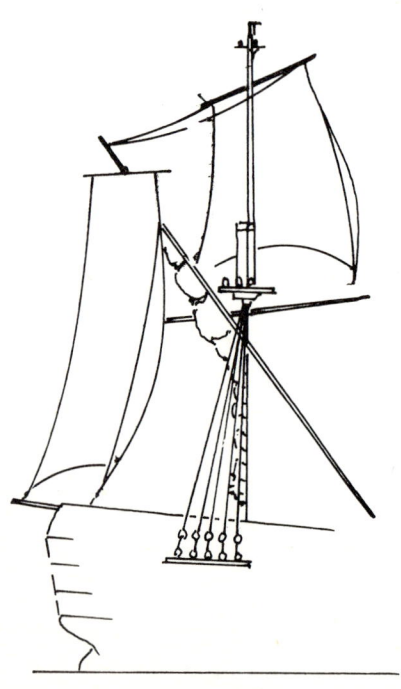

FIGURE 14

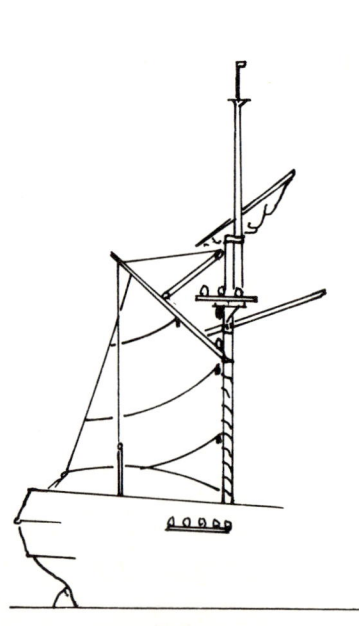

FIGURE 15

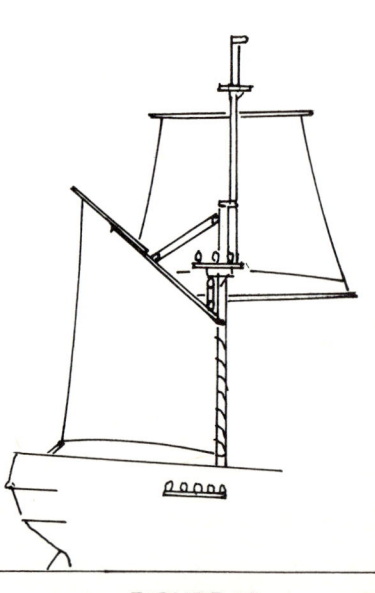

FIGURE 16

gaff, its peak initially continued to be used as a lead point for the upper mizzen yard braces, but quite early in the 19th century these braces were led forward towards the main.

Figure 14 shows a fair-weather sail used in the mid-18th century which Falconer calls a 'driver'. Its short yard was hoisted to the peak and its clews to the poop and to a boom projecting outboard on the lee side.

The first style of gaff sail was loose-footed like that found in the Stuart yachts (Figure 15) and was still described as a mizzen course. Its gaff was comparatively short; but at the turn of the 18th century the sail area was strangely increased by an extension yard (Figure 16). D'Arcey Lever described this sail as a 'spanker or driver' in 1808 but it was then probably already outdated, for the gaff sail had come into its own a decade earlier and had been considerably altered in shape. The gaff was longer and the foot was extended by a boom projecting well beyond the stern (Figure 17). This

had the interesting effect of making it necessary to hoist the ensign to the peak of the gaff in action, rather than from the tall ensign staff whence it had been flown for so long. This change seems to have started in the late 1700s, for while Mazell's engraving of the *Battle of the Saints* 1782 shows Rodney's *Formidable* with her ensign on the ensign staff, Dodd's aquatint of the *Battle of St Vincent* 1797 has every British ship with an ensign at the peak. The clew of this gaff sail was held to the extremity of the boom by an outhaul tackle, cast off when the sail was furled (by brails) and the luff was laced to the mizzen lower mast. The gaff therefore functioned as a fixed spar, although it was furnished with jaws and throat and peak halyards and so could be lowered to the deck if circumstances so demanded. Unlike the clew, the peak was secured to the outer extremity of the gaff and in consequence the brails led in a direction such that, when it was furled, they still drew it towards the yard and the throat, as they had done

on earlier mizzen courses.

In merchantmen the gaff was often lowered to furl the sail, which was then held to the mizzen lower mast by hoops along its luff. This furled state is well shown by T G Dutton in his lovely lithograph of the barque *Constance* running under reduced canvas in 1849.

Irrespective of the style of furling, once the gaff sail had become established, spread between its upper and lower spars, its own studding sail naturally followed. This took the form of an extension, laced between two yards, one projecting from the boom and the other hoisted to the peak. Lever calls this a 'driver' — after the earlier driver, no doubt — but later it was generally referred to as a 'ringtail' and was a more or less standard 'flying kite' in the clipper ships (Figure 18).

Whether the gaff was 'standing' or otherwise depended on a number of factors. A spar that was habitually lowered would naturally reduce top-weight in bad weather, while the fixed variety allowed for quick

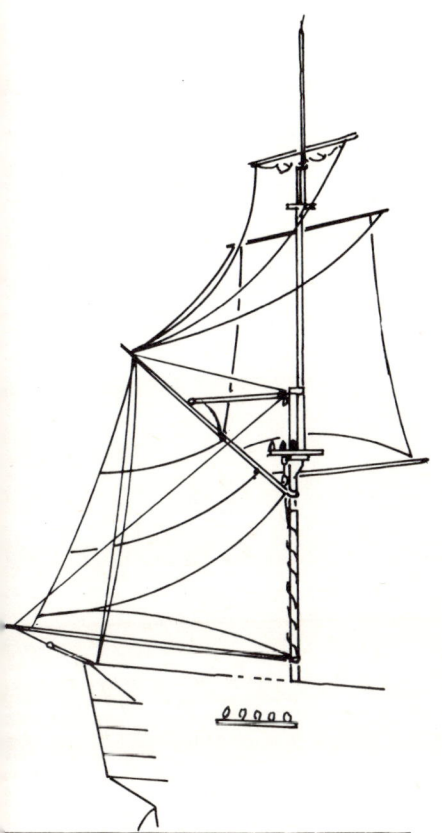

FIGURE 17

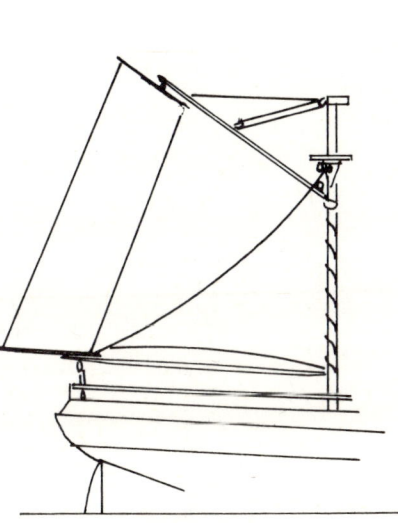

FIGURE 18

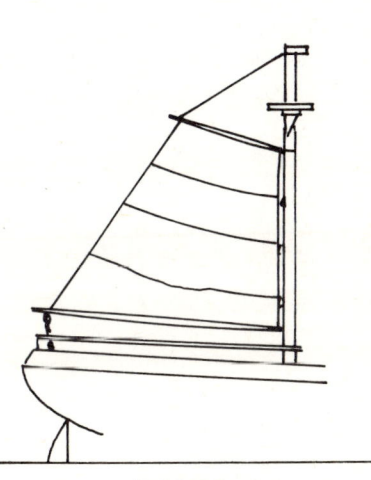

FIGURE 19

45

stowage of the sail by brails; but sometimes, in vessels with more than one gaff-headed sail, both types were employed. When *Cutty Sark* was re-rigged as a barquentine after her dismasting off South Africa, for example, she was given a standing main gaff and a lowering mizzen. Her main gaff was very large and it was probably more convenient to furl it by brails than by lowering it. However, a disadvantage of the standing gaff sail was that it could not easily be reefed, and it was thus infrequently met with in small coasting vessels — like schooners and brigantines — where its relative importance in terms of sail area and balance was more important.

Standing gaffs were rigged differently from those that were lowered. Instead of the familiar peak halyard, throat halyard, and topping lift, (running from the clew to the trestle-trees) the fixed gaff had a simple span running from peak to lower mast cap; and the boom was supported by a similar span rigged to the under side of the peak. Its gaff sail was laced to a jackstay fixed to

the after face of the mizzen mast, and had a peak outhaul in addition to the already established clew outhaul. The head of the sail ran either on tracks on a jackstay, or was hooped to the gaff, and the brails ran more or less parallel to the deck drawing the sail, like a curtain, towards the mast. This 'lie' of the brails was a sure sign that there was a peak outhaul: when the peak of the sail was seized to the end of the gaff, the brails always led towards the general area of the throat (compare Figure 19 with Figures 13,15 and 17). In the first few decades of the 19th century sail plans describe this mizzen gaff sail as either a 'driver' or a 'spanker' — the former designation being more usual in the Royal Navy, while the merchant service seem to have favoured the latter. The fact that commercial sail survived the longer probably accounts for the present acceptance of 'spanker' although it is generally unwise to set too much store on matters of precise terminology in an age when one man's shovel was another man's spade and one man's hermaphrodite

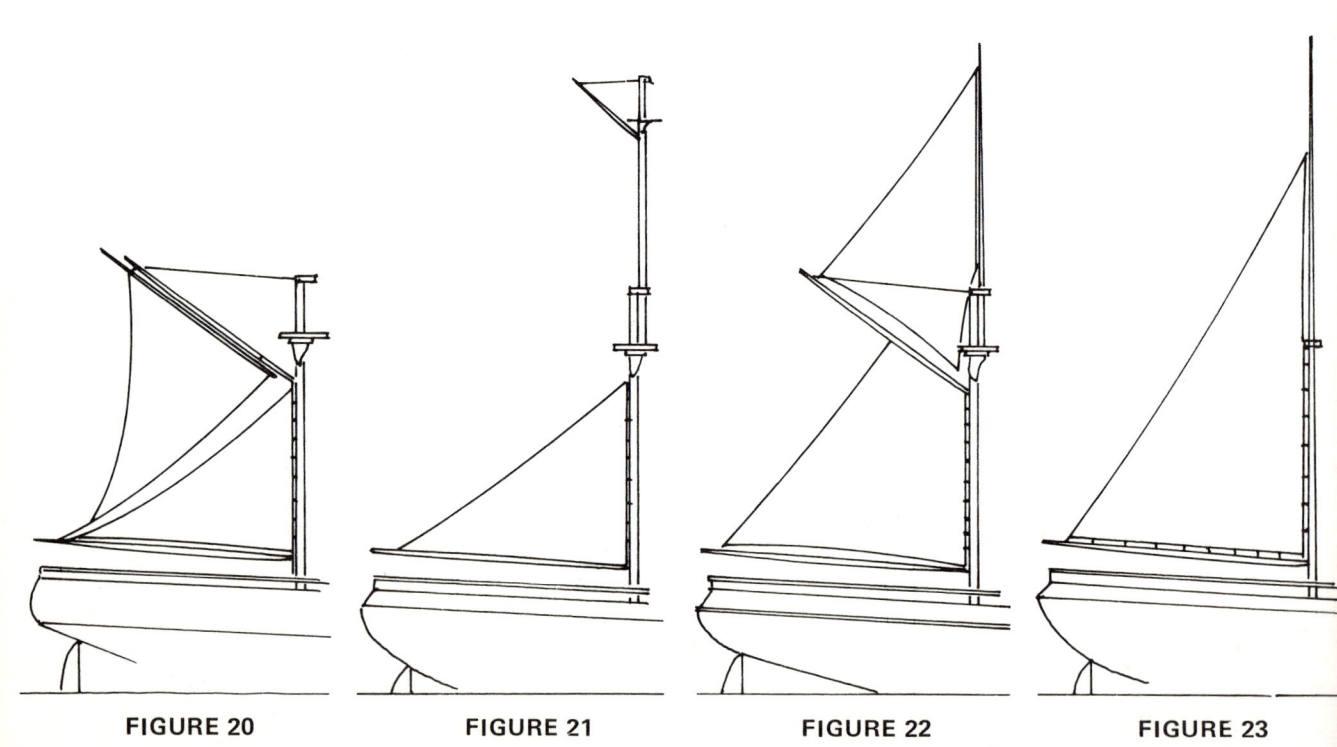

FIGURE 20   **FIGURE 21**   **FIGURE 22**   **FIGURE 23**

brig was another's brigantine.

Towards the end of the ocean-going sailing ship era the standing gaff, working in a gooseneck fitting like the boom, became the normal form. With the reduction in crews, the 'doubling' of first topsails and then topgallants leading eventually to the austere 'bald-headed' rig of the late 19th and early 20th centuries, the styles of mizzen sails were many and various and indicative of the economic strictures of the day.

Some, like the American ship *Charles E Moody* of 1882, had disproportionately short gaffs almost parallel with the boom (Figure 19), while the British four masted barque *Drummuir*, built in the same year, had a handy arrangement of trysail and triangular ringtail (Figure 20). Others dispensed with the true gaff altogether in favour of a triangular trysail, as set by the British *Largiemore* of 1892. To provide a point for ensign or signal halyards, such ships usually had a short 'monkey gaff' projecting from the mizzen cross trees (or from the jigger in the case of the four masters) (Figure 21).

Barque-rigged vessels often adopted special styles so that they could still spread a conventional jib-headed topsail on a full length gaff, but with a spanker of reduced head beneath. The American *Golden Gate* of 1888 had this arrangement (Figure 22). In 1893, the British-built four masted barque *Royal Firth* sported a trysail of almost Bermudian proportions on a tall pole jigger mast (Figure 23); and the remarkable six masted barquentine *E R Stirling* (whose masts were designated fore, main, mizzen spanker, jigger, and driver) set gaff sails on the main to jigger, a trysail on the driver, and a strange jib-headed topsail above it (Figure 24). This arrangement was also much favoured among coastal brigantines and their kin, obviating as it did (in their case) the need to hoist a heavy main gaff when the number of crew had been pared to the bone.

Herzogin Cecilie, a four masted barque of the early 20th century had the double gaff typical of German-built ships (Figure 25) and of all the compromises in the cut of spankers this was certainly one of the most attractive.

If the double gaff typified the German Laeisz fleet so, too, did the oddly split jib-headed topsails of the French barques running for A D Bordes (Figure 26). Quite what benefit was gained from this division of the topsail, cut along the old line of the peak halyards, is difficult to imagine, but it apparently had some merit for.it was often the only canvas set on the jigger mast.

While it is of course true that over the centuries the square sails of ocean-going vessels were themselves considerably modified (and some like the spritsail, and its frail partner the sprit-topsail, disappeared altogether) no other sail was subjected to more modifications and none progressed so steadily from considerable complication to singular simplicity than did the aftermost canvas of the sailing ship, where its very presence was a fundamental feature for some five hundred years.

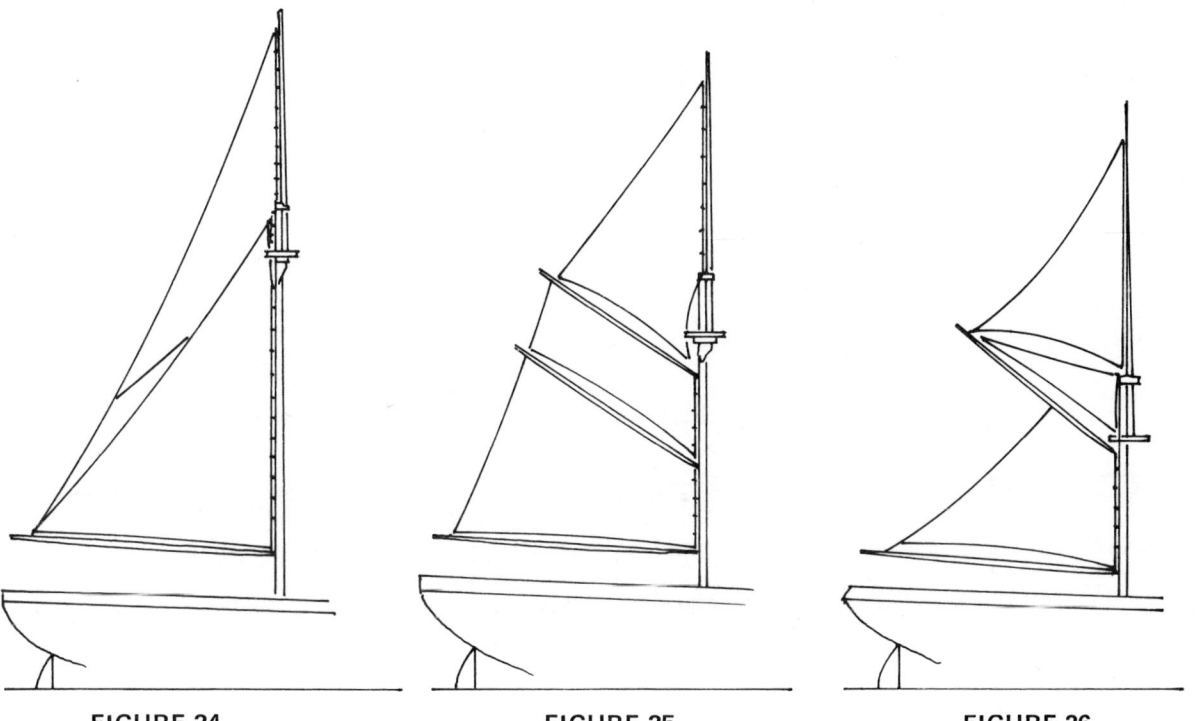

FIGURE 24　　　　　　**FIGURE 25**　　　　　　**FIGURE 26**

BLUE FUNNEL CARGO LINER
MACHAON CONCLUSION

by Geoff Michell

By the end of the last article I had covered the preparation of the midship superstructure and the fitting and detailing of the poop house. The next major job I tackled was the construction of the four winch houses. I made these out of 0.008 inch polystyrene, the thicker material making it easier to round off the corners. No 1 house was positioned between the two hatches on the well deck forward. The sides of the overhanging deck on this house tapered slightly, being wider aft than forward, and there was a recess in the deck on the centre line at each end in which was fitted the lead block for the wire rope used to open and close the hatches. This deck had the customary curtain plate around its edge, and prominent beams under the overhanging parts of the deck; these I added, using strips of plastic card to represent the flanges of the angle. Three watertight doors were fitted each side of the house. At this point I sprayed the house and underside of the deck and the curtain plate white, and the bare steel deck red.

As soon as the paint was dry I added the detail. This comprised a three bar rail all round with an opening each side in way of the vertical steel ladder, the clips and hinges on the watertight doors, the vertical steel ladders, the four winches mounted on 4 in deep channels welded to the deck, together with their control units with their protective 'cages', the mast table drilled to take the mast,

the heel fitting for the jumbo derrick, sundry small mushroom ventilators, four small bollards for use with the winches, two wire cable reels, the crutches to support the ends of the derricks from the adjacent samson posts, and sundry other small fittings.

No 4 house in the after well deck was generally similar, except that the sides were parallel, there was no heel fitting for the jumbo derrick, and there were three tall mushroom ventilators by the mast.

The front of No 2 house, at the fore end of the centre castle, was flush with the fore end of this structure, and of the same radius. The deck on the house overhung the after end of the house, and at each side it was extended to, and tapered in to meet, the adjacent samson post, to which it was (later) secured; the edge was fitted with a curtain plate. An opening had to be cut in each side to clear the steel ladder running up the inboard side of the samson posts, and there was a recess in the after end on the centre line for the hatch wire lead block. The guard rail all round was of the two bar type, and there was a single bar rail round that opening in way of the samson post ladders. The detail on the house top included four winches, each with controller unit and protective cage, two tall mushroom-topped ventilators with wire stays, two square and several round gooseneck ventilators, and derrick crutches.

No 3 house was generally similar to No 2, except that it was rectangular, and the deck overhung the sides of the house all round. Once these houses were finished I

Top: No 1 masthouse. Note: On the forecastle the two blocks at the top of the samson post and the ladder up its fore side. In the well deck the extensions to the hatch coamings, the ladder and the supports to the deck on the masthouse. On this deck the mast table, the heel fitting for the jumbo derrick and the securing clamp half way up the mast for this derrick.

Centre: Nos 2 & 3 masthouses. Note the extension of the deck on the houses to the samson posts, the derrick stowage bracket on No 6 post, the tall mushroom vents on each house and the cowl vents

Bottom: No 4 masthouse, where the 'cages' over the winch controllers are clearly seen, and just visible are the three mushroom vents by the mast table. Note the stowage of the derrick from No 9 (starboard) samson post across the corner of the poop house.

did not mount them on the model, but put them aside and turned to the next job.

HATCHES

These were of the Macgregor sliding steel cover type. Nos 2, 3, 4, and 5 were all the same width, No 2 had five covers, the others four each. No 1 also had four covers, but was narrower than the others. The side coamings of each hatch were extended fore and aft to the adjacent house, and each increased slightly in height between the cross coaming and the deckhouse, that is, under the overhanging part of the masthouse deck. Each cover unit is fitted with two cast steel wheels on each side which run in a channel trackway attached to the side coaming. Each cover in turn is connected to its neighbour by a short length of chain secured to the end of the pin through a third wheel located on a bracket welded to the top edge of the cover.

In operation, a wire attached to the end cover is passed through the previously mentioned lead block in the recess in the overhanging deck of the masthouse, and passed to a winch from where it is wound in. In so doing the hatch covers are drawn along the rails, then up the raised part of the coaming extension to pivot through 90° and stow vertically one behind the other in the space between the cross coaming and the deckhouse. When in the closed position the covers are secured by a series of steel wedges knocked home between lugs spaced along the joint between each section. I used polystyrene sheet of various

thicknesses to make the hatches and fittings, and included as much detail as possible — wheels, chain, lugs, supporting brackets to the coamings, trackway, ramps, steps, and so on. When completed, I sprayed them grey.

MIDSHIP STRUCTURE

After finishing the masthouses and hatches, I decided that the time had come to assemble the midship accommodation. Having sprayed all the units white, and painted the deckheads and the inside of the bridge wings light green, I added clear window strip to the inside of each window. Some of these I painted green to represent drawn blinds, just to give a little variation in appearance. I drilled all the holes for the rails, but only added the rails themselves as the decks were built up, the reason for this being that the rails had to be joined at various stages to the stanchions between the deck and deck above. I inserted all the portholes in 'A' deckhouse, fitted the teak capping rail to the bulwark, and added any other detail that could not be put on once the decks were permanently in position.

I now glued 'A' deck in place, taking the added precaution of fitting a fine brass screw through the deck top. I went on to fit the various stanchions in position, making the flat steel plate type below the davit trackways, and also those at the after end, from thin polystyrene strip, with the correct strip on the inboard side. The radius at the top I cut as part of the stanchion, but the brackets at the foot I added afterwards as separate pieces. The arched double stanchion at the fore end I cut in one piece. I spent a lot of time blending all these parts into the curtain plate and bulwark, as they had to present a completely smooth surface with no sign of a join. This again I achieved with thin coats of paint, each coat being gently rubbed down with small pieces of fine wet and dry until the joins were invisible. I used 0.008 in nickel silver for the stanchions, and fitted the rails along the sides and across the after end. In way of the accommodation ladder the rails are set back to provide a stowage space for the ladder. All the rails of the midship accommodation were of the four bar type. A number of small gooseneck and other ventilators were fitted along the edge of the main deck, and there was a small refuelling hose derrick each side at the forward end of this deck. Finally I added the four ladders complete with hand rails, which gave access to the centre castle deck — two ladders forward and two aft.

'B' deck came next, and I added the detail as before. One of the main differences lay in the ladder openings through the fore part of the Boat Deck where a four bar set of rails were positioned on each side of the openings. I found it very difficult to fit the ladder handrails on these owing to the confined space once the decks were in place. Outside each door, and at the top and bottom of each ladder, I glued four very small wood treadstrips to the deck. The rails on the Promenade Deck had a teak top rail all round, which joined up to the teak capping rail on the bulwark at the fore end. I made these capping rails from copper wire, producing the oval cross section by flattening it in the same way as I did for the awning spars. I glued the wire to the top of the rail stanchions and gave it a coat of teak paint.

In the case of 'C' deck I was able to fit all the rails on the after end, as well as those lengths of rail running along the deck on the inboard side of the davits, before glueing the deck in place. Incidentally, all these rails also had teak top rails. With 'C' deck in place, I was able to fit and glue the davits, taking care that they were aligned correctly with the plate stanchions below, and add the rails which ran between the davit trackways.

Before fitting the wheelhouse unit in place I added the binnacle, wheel, flag locker and sundry cupboards. As I mentioned before, the doors to the wheelhouse were left in the open position to give a clear view of the interior. On the outside of the two outer windows on the front of the wheelhouse I fitted two small clear plastic discs to represent the clearview spinning discs, and fitted a small brass bell above the central window of the wheelhouse. My method of joining the wheelhouse front section to the bridge wings

worked out very well; once glued in place, I only had to give a little rub with wet and dry and a touch of paint to produce a satisfactory join. The final deck unit, that section which was 2 ft above the deck, I now glued in place. However, before doing any more detail work on it, I decided to make the last of the major parts for the model.

SAMSON POSTS

The ten samson posts were all the same diameter but varied a little in length according to their position. I used polystyrene rod for these, turning it down to 0.12 in diameter at the base, then tapering each post just over one degree over its full length. At the bottom I formed the usual spigot for fitting into the deck. There were only minor differences in detail on the posts. For instance, Nos 1 and 2, situated on the forecastle, had swivel mountings for one derrick each, whereas all the others had two, one on each side. Nos 9 and 10, on the poop deck, had square ventilator trunking with a cap on top running half way up the inboard side. The vertical ladders, which stopped just short of the top, posed quite a problem at first. Then I hit on the idea of making them out of fine mesh curtain net. After hunting around in a number of drapers' shops — not without a certain amount of embarrasment I might add, especially when announcing that I only wanted about a square foot of the stuff — I found a perfect scale mesh after searching through quite a selection, and the sales girl actually give it to me when I told her how I was going to use it!

First I made a simple wood frame about 4 in x 3 in, then placed a piece of the net over the frame, securing it in place with a strong elastic band round the outside of the frame. After pulling the mesh exactly square I brushed on a fairly thin coat of Cascamite glue, taking care to get rid of any blobs before it set. Once set the glue served a double purpose — it not only stiffened the net, but also secured each strand, which was so essential for the next step. This

entailed laying the net on a flat cutting surface, and cutting with a sharp razor and a steel rule single ladder lengths, taking care to cut exactly on the outside of the vertical strand so as not to leave the ends of cross strands showing. Next I cut straight lengths of 0.007 in diameter copper wire to the correct length after both the ends had been turned over a right angles and cut off short. These pieces of wire were then glued with Seccotine, one on either side, to each of the strips of cut net. With some patience and a lot of time, I was able to produce very realistic scale ladders. All the vertical ladders on the model were made in this way — and there were many of them.

To return to the samson post detail. All the derrick heel fittings (swivels) were produced in full detail, including a small hole to take the pin of the fitting on the end of the derrick. At the top of the post I fitted the mountings for the topping lift blocks, the blocks themselves being added later. Having done this I sprayed them with the brown mast colour, except for Nos 7 and 8,

situated at the after end of the Boat Deck, which I sprayed white. When the paint was dry I added the rest of the detail which included three thin wire rings set slightly clear of the post and used as foot rungs when working aloft, two small block hoists on the top, cargo working lights, steel ladders, and on some the crutches for securing the ends of adjacent derricks in the stowed position. All this detail I painted by hand.

MASTS

I turned the two masts from polystyrene rod.but, owing to their length and the changing taper ending in a very small diameter section at the top, I found them difficult to produce satisfactorily. I fed the rod slowly out of the collet, cutting the taper with a tool bit but doing quite a lot of the shaping with a fine file, before finishing off with wet and dry. The crosstrees I built up with polystyrene in order to get the correct hollow effect on the underside, and piercing the four oval holes on each face. The foremast had

a length of ventilation trunking on the fore side, and a heavy clamp about half way up the after side to secure the jumbo derrick in its stowed position. As with the samson posts, I sprayed both masts the brown mast colour before going on to add the fine detail, which included such items as the truck at the top, brackets for the masthead lights, the cargo lights, several fine wire rings as on the samson posts, and a couple of folding arms to take cargo light clusters. On the crosstrees there was a single bar guard rail, and four mountings to take the derrick topping lift blocks. The steel ladders, in several lengths, ran up the masts on the fore side as far as the crosstrees, and from there to the top on the side of the mast.

DERRICKS

There were 28 derricks in all, made up as follows:- 18 five ton SWL (safe working load), 1 seven ton, 8 ten ton, and 1 thirty-five ton jumbo. These varied in length and diameter. I used nickel silver rod to start with, turning down to 0.018 in for the swivel pin, and reducing the diameter by a few thou' at either end with a double step to represent the 'telescopic' appearance of the construction of the derricks. The jumbo had several large lugs on either side at the top, and an increase in diameter at the base. I left this derrick in the unrigged state, as the rigging (blocks and so on) is usually only rigged when they are needed for special heavy lifts. I sprayed all the derricks mast brown, except for the 2 five ton and 1 seven ton fitted to the samson posts at the after end of the Boat Deck, which were white.

RADAR MAST

The tall radar mast situated just forward of the funnel I made from nickel silver wire. This had several reduction steps in its length. Some feet below the top of the mast I fitted a circular platform. This had a double bar guard rail round it; the supporting stanchions for the rail leaned outboard from the platform, so that the upper rail was further away from the mast than the lower one. I fully detailed the radar scanner at the top of the mast, recessing the front, and fitting a wire hoop round

it and over its top. A vertical steel ladder ran from the top of the wheelhouse at its after end to the circular platform. This ladder could not be fitted until the mast was in position, as it passed between the two stays fitted between the mast and the funnel to support the mast. The whole was painted white.

FINAL ASSEMBLY

I was now able to turn to the final assembly of the model. Starting at the fore end, I glued the two samson posts in place on the forecastle, then fitted No 1 hatch and No 1 mast house, and continued working aft until all hatches, mast houses and samson posts, and masts were in place. I ought to have mentioned that the two samson posts at the after end of the Boat Deck were set with half their diameter in the side of the house.

After this I concentrated on the midship structure. The first items to go on were the funnel and the radar mast and its ladder, followed by the four boat winches with canvas covers, the complete rigging of the boat davits, including the falls and the lines attached to the wire span between the sliding arms. I made the eight tall snowdrop-shaped embarkation lights by turning a piece of nickel silver wire over the shank of a drill to form the neck, made the flat cone-shaped shade from a 0.01 in disc slipped over the end of the wire, and finished below the disc with a clear polystyrene dome-shaped turning for the lamp cover. The stem of each light was supported by a couple of wire stays secured to the stem about half-way up its length. The lights were positioned one at either end of the Boat Deck and one inboard of each boat. There were five other floodlights, one each side at the after end of the top of the wheelhouse, two abaft the funnel, and one on top of the large fan housing abaft the funnel. Four of these were on three legs with cross supports, and the lights were nearly square with a dish shaped bottom half. I glued a tiny square of chrome tape on these, which was quite effective when caught in the light. On the wheelhouse top a double row of rails ran from the monkey

island to the access ladder at the after end; these rails had a teak top rail. The only other detail here was the compass in the monkey island, a D/F loop, an all-round light on a wood post, and some small ventilators.

At the after end of the Boat Deck I fitted the two winches, complete with protective frames. The detail on the raised deck under the funnel included a steel hatch with wing nuts round the top just abaft the funnel, and which had collapsible stanchions with two rows of chain surrounding it. The rest consisted of fan units, tanks, a tall conical air intake, stowage lockers, small ventilators, and a single pair of bollards at the after end. There were also some small stowage lockers and boxes on the bridge and at the after end of the Boat Deck, and two gyro compass repeaters on the bridge wings with small gratings on the deck round the base of their pedestals. I made the port and starboard navigation lights of brass, glueing them into the light boxes fixed outside the ends of the bridge wings. On the after side of each bridge wing I fitted a lifebuoy in its quick release stowage. The two ladders from the bridge to the Boat Deck came directly over the openings in that deck for the two ladders leading to the deck below. Also on the bridge and on the Boat Deck was an extensive arrangement of awning stanchions and rafters, which I made in the same way as those on the poop. I fitted the two accommodation ladders and showed the starboard one in the stowed position, and the port one in the turned out position all set for being lowered into place. In this position all the stanchions and ropes are in place, but the treads (steps) are lying flat, only moving into position when the ladder is lowered. I left the bottom extension lashed inboard on two chocks, but the hinged arm with the block and tackle and bridle and chains are all in place. By showing the starboard ladder in the stowed position I was able to include all the diagonal rods and mechanism required to alter the tread angle fitted to the underside of the ladder, together with the hinged steel grating which formed the top platform and which was stowed vertically.

I arranged the derricks in both the stowed and raised (working) positions. The three stowed on Nos 7 and 8 samson posts were stowed athwartship and crossing at a slightly raised angle, whilst the two forward of the bridge for working No 4 hatch were stowed fore and aft; their heel fitting was on the face of the bulwark at the fore end of the Promenade deck, with the upper end of the derrick resting on a crutch on the outboard side of Nos 5 and 6 samson posts respectively. The two serving the small double hatch on the poop were shown with the starboard derrick stowed diagonally across the corner of the house on the poop, and the port one raised. The remainder were stowed in either of these two conditions. The method of

Below: No 4 hatch, taken on board the ship and showing the coaming stays, the channel trackway, the two different sets of wheels on the hatch covers, the upper ones carrying the short chains connecting the hatch covers.

fixing was simply by bending the pin formed at the end of the derrick to the correct angle and glueing it into its swivel mounting on mast table or samson post. All the derrick crutches were fitted with rope lashings hanging down. Incidentally, I was surprised to see that this ship still used rope lashings rather than the more conventional steel clamp with securing pin.

My next task on the derricks was to make the dozens of topping lift, lead and runner blocks, in most cases six for each derrick. Nos 1 and 2 on the forecastle are typical. Starting with the blocks for the topping lift there is one double at the derrick head, two singles at the top of the samson post set a few feet apart, and one single lead block shackled to an eyeplate at the foot of the post. The cargo runner had a single block at the derrick head, and a single attached to the heel swivel mounting on the samson post. These steel blocks were round, with a flat tail attached, and were all of the same diameter, but of course the doubles

were thicker, and the single lead blocks were minus the tail. I made the sheaves from polystyrene rod, turned to size and parted off, then glued on the tails where appropriate. Starting with No 1 derrick I glued each block in position so that it sat at the correct angle in its rigged state. I used a length of straight steel wire as an aid to determining the angle of the rigging in relation to each block. I gave the blocks a coat of black paint prior to fixing, and touched up with paint afterwards where necessary and finally, after rigging, applied a thin coat of matt varnish, with a touch at all glue points to take away any tell-tale glossy spots and also act as a sealer. Another job I had to do before starting on the actual rigging of the model was to make and fit dozens of tiny ring bolts and cleats along the bulwark capping, and on the deckhouses and decks. Although very small at this scale — I made them of 0.004 in diameter copper wire — they did give a finished touch, as I was able to bring the guy ropes to the

cleats, and fit the lower guy blocks to the ring bolts. I made the ring bolts in the usual way by winding a length of the wire round the shank of a suitable size of twist drill, cutting off each turn and pressing them flat. The rigging proved to be a long and exacting job, as I had decided that I would include every piece. I was only able to do this since the Blue Funnel Line had very kindly let me have the use of a complete rigging plan. I chose copper wire (0.002 in diameter) for the rigging, as it had the merit of being unaffected by atmospheric conditions, and to my mind looks more authentic when used to represent wire rope. Having said that, I must add that I did use terylene for the mooring ropes, glueing the coils and leaving a large loop at one end.

First I had to colour the wire. I wound a length of the copper wire lengthways round the frame used for the net ladders, carefully taking out some of the stretch while so doing. I found that about ten turns at a time were sufficient, and secured the ends with plasticine. I then gave them a thin coat of Humbrol black: with a little practice I found I could get good results with a minimum thickness and no blobs. After cutting away the straight pieces from the frame and giving each length a further stretch with two pairs of pliers, I cut the usable lengths from these pieces. Even after all this I found it necessary to give each a final roll with a steel rule on a sheet of glass. I also used this wire for the guy ropes, and these I painted 'rope' colour. Where I needed very long pieces, as for the wireless aerials, forestay, and so on, I stretched out a length of wire on a sheet of paper, and drew them through a paint impregnated brush, which proved to be very effective.

The principle I used to rig the model consisted of cutting pieces of the wire to the exact length required and glueing them in place; there is no reeving, knotting, etc, on the model. It is most important to work from the centre outwards, and starting with those derricks in the raised position. I began with the topping lifts. Each strand was cut to bring it to the centre line of the block. On the double blocks where there were

four pieces of wire, I had to take great care to keep all the wires from touching one another. On the single purchase blocks there was one strand top and bottom, with the third strand starting in the centre. My idea, of course, was to create the impression that the wire passed continuously through the blocks. The single part (downhaul) then passed through two lead blocks to be made fast on the bitts near the winch; each part of this lead was a separate piece of wire, as before. The cargo runners varied, some being single and some double with an extra block; they ran from the head of the derrick through a lead block fitted to the derrick heel fitting to the centre drum on the winch. I found the guys and pennants an exacting and time consuming task. The only way I found that these could be represented successfully was to work out the required distance between the two blocks, then glue them temporarily on a sheet of material this distance apart. Next I added the wire pennant to the upper block and the two rope-coloured pieces of wire between the blocks. Once the guys had set I put them in position and added the hauling strand to the double block at the top, the end being secured to a cleat. The single block guys were simpler, having only two strands, one going to a cleat and the other to a ring bolt. This was a job where the paint brush and seccotine method worked to good advantage, as I was able to reduce the contacts points to a minimal size. I attached a coiled-up tail of rope to each guy, making these by winding some wire round a drill shank, glueing and forming into oval shapes, and bending some so that they could hang over the bulwark capping rail. Once in place I gave each a touch of paint.

I found the derricks in the stowed position a little easier, since the guys and runners were stowed underneath. Although a lot of the detail on the inboard derricks was lost to view, I carefully included every piece. On the other hand the topping lifts entailed more setting up owing to the very long lengths required, the need to keep them apart, and at the same time having to see that they sagged just that right amount. I also

found some difficulty with the three derricks stowed athwartship at the after end of the Boat Deck owing to the lack of working space, and the fact that quite a number of the strands crossed each other. As I mentioned, the guys are stowed below the derricks, usually by shackling the end block to a point at the derrick base, hauling taut, then jamming the block with the hauling part, coiling the spare rope over the guy, and finishing with two half hitches to secure the coil. I made the coils in the same way as before, but preformed them to the correct shape by nipping them with tweezers. Once glued into position over the guys and adjusted, they looked very realistic.

The remainder of the rigging consisted of a stay from the top of the foremast down to the forecastle at the stem, a signal halyard span from the foremast head to the fore side of the funnel — passing through a small block on the mast and on the funnel — and having four pairs of signal halyards attached to it, these halyards running down to the bridge wings. Another similar span ran from the mainmast head to the after side of the funnel to take the various wireless aerials. An emergency aerial ran from the funnel to the top of No 8 samson post; this was the one on the port side, and the aerial was attached to a small bracket at the top of the funnel on the port side. The last wire I added was the main aerial running from mast to mast, and which was, of course, the longest piece of wire on the model. Its halyards ran through a block at each end on the mast, which I had already attached, down to their cleat at the foot of the mast. I represented the insulators with tiny blobs of seccotine painted white. There were quite a number of small ropes and wires on the model, all of which I put on by one or other of the methods I have just described.

The last detail I added was the flags — the Red Ensign at the stern, the House Flag at the mainmast head, and three international code signal flags flying from the bridge halyards. These were Q (yellow) meaning 'my vessel is healthy', H (white and red vertical) meaning 'I have a pilot on board' and J (blue with white horizontal band through the centre) meaning 'I am going to send a message by semaphore'. I chose these three signal letters as the general appearance of my model suggests that she is entering port – hence the gangway on the side unshipped and ready for lowering, some derricks up ready for working cargo, and mooring ropes ready on the forecastle. I made the flags from rice paper, painted on each side with watercolour paints, creased and formed into wind-blown folds. I attached each to the halyards with a tiny spot of glue on the corners.

The model was now complete, and all that remained for me to do was to mount it in the glass case. As I mentioned earlier, I had made provision for mounting it on two turned brass pillars, which when fitted gave a clearance of just under an inch between the keel and the baseboard. When turning the pillars I formed a step at each end, the lower one being threaded. This end passed through a 5/8 in oblong teak baseboard, where it was secured with a nut in a recess on the underside. This baseboard in turn fitted into a well in the base of the glass case, where it fastened with two screws put in from the underside. As a finishing touch I glued some blue baize, almost the shade of the Blue Funnel blue, round the teak stand to form a border to the base. I felt that this set the model off rather well.

I would just like to finish by expressing my thanks to the Blue Funnel Line for all the assistance which they gave me, to Mr T Carfrae and Mr A Humphreys who came with me on my two visits to the ship and whose photographs covering every part of the ship were of inestimable help, and without which I could not have incorporated so much accurate detail in the model, to Mr E Wilson for much help with this article, and finally to my very patient wife for putting up with the many hours I spent working on the model during the fourteen years it was under construction, and wondering if it would ever be completed!

At the Model Engineer Exhibition in London in January Geoff Michell received the premier award, the Duke of Edinburgh Challenge Trophy, for this model. We are sure that readers will join us in congratulating Geoff on this magnificent culmination to his years of painstaking work.

Below: The midship structure, showing in particular the radar mast and its supports on to the funnel, the fittings on the top of the wheelhouse, the lights abreast each lifeboat, and the brackets top and bottom of the wide plate stanchions below the davits.

In the absence of any title relating to ship modelling specifically, we feel justified in devoting space to some of our own titles that will be of more interest to modelmakers than most.

The names of the American historians Howard Chapelle, Charles G Davis and F Alexander Magoun will be known to many readers, but their works are difficult to obtain, particularly in Europe and the UK. Therefore Conway Maritime is distributing US-produced large format reprints of *The Baltimore Clipper, Ships of the Past* and *The Frigate Constitution and other Historic Ships*. Taking this last first: Magoun was a naval architect at the Massachusetts Institute of Technology who drew up the plans for the restoration of the *Constitution*. His book is largely given over to this frigate in all her details, with a full set of plans and diagrams, but it also contains a similar combination of reconstructed plans and background information for Viking ships (based on the Gokstad ship), the *Santa Maria, Mayflower,* clipper *Flying Cloud* and the schooner *Bluenose*.

Charles G Davis' *Ships of the Past* also devotes chapters to particular types ranging from coastal craft and fishing schooners to Baltimore clippers, the packet *Isaac Webb* and the frigates *Raleigh* and *Congress*. Besides being profusely illustrated, the work has appendices on masting and sparring, and on sources for plans of ships.

The Baltimore Clipper was one of Chapelle's first works but his distinctive approach, combining naval architecture and history, is

Photos: on board views from the author's collection, model photos by John Bowen

model Shipwright

THE FIRST FOUR ISSUES

We are pleased to announce that we are reprinting the first four issues of **Model Shipwright** in response to requests from our many new subscribers. Undertaken in association with our North American subscription agents, Ship Modelers Associates, this strictly limited edition will present the four issues in a single, prestigious case-bound volume.

The contents of **Volume I** include:

The first 4 parts of Ewart Freeston's detailed description of building a 17th century dockyard model.

George Osborn's articles on the introduction of steam into the Royal Navy, still the only authoritative published material on this period.

A series on waterline miniatures by John Bowen.

The first of P N Thomas' 'Ships That Served'.

Features by such well-known maritime historians as Basil Greenhill, Michael Bouquet, Alex Hurst and Antony Preston.

Information on tools and materials, news of museums book reviews, 'Photo Album' and readers' letters.

A total of 392 pages including index, many photos, diagrams and plans.

Availability
July 1978, but please order quickly as the print run is strictly limited and customers will be supplied on a 'first come, first served' basis.

USA and Canada Available only from:
Ship Modelers Associates
38 Hartford Avenue
Wethersfield
Connecticut 06109
USA.

Price: $25 (plus $1 postage in USA;
$1.50 in Canada)

UK and the rest of the world from:
Conway Maritime Press Ltd
2 Nelson Road
Greenwich
London SE10 9JB
UK

Price: £12 (plus 50p postage)

already apparent. As usual the book incorporates many of the author's fine plans, and forty years after it was first published it is still the best available study of these craft.

Each of the above is 10 1/3 x 8¼ in, of about 180 - 200 pages, and is priced at £5.50 (plus 50p postage) per volume. Available from Conway Maritime Press Ltd..

Jean Boudriot's magnificent *Le Vaisseau de 74 Canons* is another book that is difficult to obtain outside its country of origin, but Meridian Books (at the same address as Conway Maritime, 2 Nelson Road, London SE10 9JB) have a limited stock of Volumes III and IV. These cover masting and rigging (Vol III) and manning, seamanship, manoeuvres under sail and tactics (Vol IV) and are the only volumes currently available. For those who wish to complete an imposing but expensive set, the price is £35 (plus £2.00 postage) per volume. (We hope to include a fuller review of these volumes in the next issue.)

RECENT PUBLICATIONS

As usual maritime publications this spring have been dominated by naval titles. One of the most impressively produced was *Fast Fighting Boats* (Nautical Publishing £19.50) in the same series and format as MacGregor's *Fast Sailing Ships.* This is a translation of two of the three volumes of Fock's German work, the English work covering 1870 - 1945 and omitting the post-war developments. This is obviously an area of increasing interest, since Macdonald

recently published *Fast Attack Craft* by Phelan and Brice, and later this year (July £12) there will be a *Brassey's Fast Attack Craft* from Seeley Service. Nautical, however, have dropped all references to Ballard's *Black Battlefleet.*

Patrick Stephens Ltd have a number of interesting imports from the US, including *A Battle History of the Imperial Japanese Navy 1941 - 1945* (£13.95) by Paul S Dull, and a second, revised edition of the *Guide to the Soviet Navy* (£13.95) by Siegfried Breyer and Norman Polmar. Devotees of the fascinating *Mariners' Catalog* will note that Volume 5 is now available at £6.50.

Seeley Service have undertaken the English edition of Stephan Terzibaschitsch's German book as *Battleships of the US Navy in WWII* (£9.95); Ian Allan's *Cruisers at War* by Gregory Haines (£6.95) is the first naval title in their pictorial 'at war' series; and the list of naval publications is rounded off by Conway Maritime's *Camera at Sea 1939 - 1945* (£12.00), a collection of the best photography of the war at sea.

Batsford continue their seemingly interminable photographic series with *Victorian and Edwardian Yachting in Old Photographs* (£4.50) by Mark Harper, and *Ships and Harbours from Early Photographs* (£4.95) by Basil Greenhill and Ann Gifford.

Hamlyn's Spring books included one unusual item: *The Country Life Book of Nautical Terms under Sail,* which could be a valuable, if costly, addition to a modeller's library (£15.00).

Merchant ships, as ever, are the poor relations of maritime publishing, but one very useful book has been released recently – *Comecon Merchant Ships* (£4.00) by Ambrose Greenway, published by Kenneth Mason, which is an identification manual of Communist shipping.

Finally, there is an interesting item in the form of a pictorial history of canal boats, called *The Narrow Boat Book* by Tom Chaplin (Whittet Books £7.50 or £4.95 paperback).

FUTURE PUBLICATIONS

Conway's own Autumn programme includes the second title, *Scale Model Warships,* in a series begun so successfully with *Scale Model Sailing Ships; The Last of the Tall Ships* is a highly illustrated book on the fleet of sailing ships built up by Gustav Erikson, a Finnish shipowner who bought sailing tonnage when everybody else was rapidly selling up. A major event for warship enthusiasts will be the publication of *Conway's All the World's Fighting Ships 1860 - 1905,* the first complete listing of all major warships built between the *Warrior* and the *Dreadnought,* with 400 photos and 500 line drawings.

CLASSIC SHIPS NO.3

ENDEAVOUR

by R A Lightley

Bob Lightley will be familiar to regular subscribers for his magnificent series about his bomb ketch 'Granado', which won the first National Maritime Museum modelmaking competition. Following this success, he was commissioned by the Museum to build a cutaway model of Cook's 'Endeavour'. This apparently well documented ship caused him many problems, and the following article incorporates the more interesting conclusions from his extensive research.

'At two pm got under sail and put to sea having on board 94 persons including officers, seamen, Gentlemen and their servants, near 18 months provisions, 10 carriage guns, 12 swivels with good store of ammunition and stores of all kinds...' This was Captain James Cook's entry in the *Endeavour's* journal on Friday 26 August 1768.

Although a King's ship, the *Endeavour* was not a man-of-war. She was in fact a lowly ex-collier bark converted to survey vessel. In 1771, her task completed and being considered of no great importance, she was converted to store ship and thereafter made three voyages to the Falkland Islands. She then disappears from written history after being sold from Service on 17 March 1775 for £645. It is believed, however, that she sailed again as a collier in the North Sea and ended her days at Newport, Rhode Island, after running aground there.

It was the importance of Captain Cook's incomparable contribution

to navigation that led to posterity granting a permanent place in history to his first command. The *Endeavour* is a ship which has caused the imagination of many modellers to reconstruct its shape in miniature form and it is fortunate that a fair amount of information is available. It seems reasonable to suppose that in view of the great interest that has been maintained to this day in the great seaman and his voyages, it is unlikely that any new material will come to light.

HISTORY

Originally built as a collier bark named the *Earl of Pembroke,* the vessel was three years old when it was taken into Admiralty service on 29 March 1768 for the price of £2307 5s 6d. Work was immediately put in hand to convert the collier into a suitable vessel to convey 94 persons and a quantity of stores on a voyage lasting three years. It is reasonable to suppose that Cook, himself an ex-collier man, had a hand in choosing a roomy ship well able to contain provisions for such a period at sea.

The purpose of the voyage was first raised in February 1768 when the Royal Society wrote to King George III requesting the fitting out of an expedition to the South Seas in order to observe the transit of Venus across the face of the sun. Instructions were later given to Cook in the form of sealed orders requiring him to search for a continent believed at that time to exist in the South Pacific.

The voyage bagan on 26 August

1768 from Plymouth. What was remarkable in this voyage was the lack of scurvy, prevented by Cook's insistence on the crew's consumption of the juice of oranges and lemons and the inclusion of *sauerkraut* in the meals. It made more tragic the epidemic which struck the vessel and its hitherto healthy crew at Batavia, when many of its officers and men died of dysentery.

The voyage to Tahiti, the ship's sojourn there, the journey to New Zealand and its circumnavigation and charting, the near disaster amongst the coral outcrops in the Great Barrier Reef, are well known and can be read in detail in most books on the subject.

The *Endeavour* arrived back in England on Saturday 13 July 1771.

DRAUGHTS

The original draughts of the conversion are available at the National Maritime Museum, Greenwich, and copies may be purchased. Commercially produced

copies of the draughts are also available. These are designed to assist less experienced modellers and generally include details not usually shown on the official drawings. Sail plans are not available in the originals although a list of spars does exist on one of the draughts. Commercially produced sail plans are probably based on these measurements.

There are, of course, plans accompanying kits which cater for the still less experienced modeller, but the plans are usually of dubious accuracy. So one is able to choose in regard to the draughts and for those who would prefer to see for themselves, the following draughts are available at the National Maritime Museum, Greenwich. It should be mentioned at this stage that a study of these draughts has revealed that two different sets are in the collection. One showing the conversion from the *Earl of Pembroke* in 1768 and the other into a storeship after the voyage in 1771.
First conversion 1768

Left top: BM, ADD MS 9345 ff 57. See Pictorial Reference.
Bottom: A view of the *Endeavour* at the entrance into the Bay of Aware.

By courtesy of The British Museum

Opposite top: The *Endeavour* at sea by Sydney Parkinson.
Centre and bottom: The *Endeavour's* boats, by the same artist.

By courtesy of Cambridge University Press; the Hakluyt Society and the British Museum

3814b Sheer draught and inboard works. The dotted lines show alterations and new work. A word of caution when using this draught. I discovered errors in the body plan (see **3814a** below). Scale 1/48.
63819b Deck plans. These are actually dated 11 July 1768 and show great detail concerning the accommodation in the 'tween decks. Scale 1/96.
3816 An enlarged copy of the officers quarters shown in **3819b**. Scale 1/48.
3818 Enlarged copy of the quarter deck shown in **3819b**. Scale 1/48.

Second Conversion 1771
3814a Sheer draught and inboard works. This is how the vessel appeared on 16 October 1771 when it was converted to a storeship for a voyage to the Falkland Islands. The lines are accurate in this draught. Scale 1/48.
3819 Deck plans. These show the arrangement of the partitions in this conversion. Spar sizes are shown on this draught. Scale 1/96.

It is noteworthy that although quarterbadge detail is shown there is no other ornamentation or any stern views. This is unusual, for when lines were taken off existing vessels it was customary to depict stern details on the draughts.

DOCUMENTS
The most valuable written document is of course Cook's journal, written between 27 May 1768 and 13 July 1771, followed by the ship's log, the First Officer's and lesser officer's journals. Then there are the Admiralty letters. These documents

are difficult of access but they have
been studied by noted scholars and
have been edited in various forms
and in books. By far the best is the
Voyage of the Endeavour, one of a
four part series on Cook's voyages
edited by J C Beaglehole and
published for the Hakluyt Society
by the Cambridge Press. This volume
is a mine of information and has in
it as much as there is to know about
the voyage. Numerous books on the
subject of Cook deal with all three
voyages, and reference to the
Endeavour is generally incidental.
There are however certain valuable
illustrations to be found in some of
these books and they are well worth
examination:
Captain Cook and the South Pacific
Oliver Warner (Cassel Caravel)
The Voyages of Captain Cook
Rex and Thea Rienits (Paul Hamlyn)
Captain Cook the Seamen's Seaman
Alan Villiers (Hodder & Stoughton)

In volume 19 of *Mariner's Mirror*
C Knight wrote a valuable
contribution by recording the survey
report of the *Earl of Pembroke*. He
includes copies of letters and writes
of the eventual fate of the ship.

PICTORIAL REFERENCE
The drawings of Sydney Parkinson,
one of the two artists on the voyage,
are preserved in the British Museum
and are treasured for their accuracy
and attention to botanical detail.
There are also four sketches of the
Endeavour which are attributed to
him.

B M, Add. MS 9345 ff 16 v shows
the *Endeavour* at sea. The vessel is
under storm sails and is of little use,
except to show general outline. A
copy of this picture may also be
seen in the Beaglehole edited journal
and in *Captain Cook and the South
Pacific.*

A picture showing the *Endeavour*
drawn up for repairs on the Australian
coast after the grounding is supposed
to have been drawn by Parkinson but
this is not certain. Dr John
Hawkesworth used the picture in his
version of the voyage. It is not of
much value except that, like all the
others, it does agree that there were
five stern windows (see *Captain Cook
and the South Pacific* (Warner),
where an etching is reproduced).

BM, Add, MS 9345 ff 57. Surely

the prize of them all. What a wealth of detail is contained in this very sketchy sketch. Clearly, the ship is lying in a tropical anchorage, possibly Tahiti, where she spent some time. The yards are sent down. An awning stretches over the quarterdeck. (I do not believe that this is the conjectural platform over the tiller referred to in the journal; it is too high above the deck). All the ports are open, allowing the free passage of air through the ship. The disposition of these ports agree very accurately with those on the draught. Even the hinging, whether at the sides or tops, is faithfully shown. The five windows are once again depicted. Note that the centre one is larger than the others. Carved flower garlands decorate the window mullions. There are clearly strange hinged shutters suspended above the windows. Even the quarter badge windows has side hung casements. For the first time here is a reference to carvings. Although the draughts show foliage on the quarter badge, nothing is shown on the quarters. The stern is not shown on the draught at all. In this drawing we see female figures on the quarters. On examination, the starboard quarter figure reveals a female elbow and hip with leg below. The port side figure, too, shows a head with body below. Foliage trails across the tafferel and a rope ladder hangs centrally below the lantern and down to the water line. For reproduction of this drawing see the *Voyages of Captain Cook* (Rienits). Truly volumes are spoken in this very valuable drawing. How grateful we are to Sydney Parkinson.

RIGGING
No model should be considered complete without rigging. There were quite important changes in the rigging of vessels of this period and unless one has access to accurate information serious anachronisms may result. Unfortunately in this instance we are scratching barren ground if looking for published material. Apart from Steele's *Mastmaking and Rigging*, which is largely too late for the *Endeavour,* Anderson's *17th Century Rigging* is far too early. D'Arcy Lever helps but is also rather after 1768.

RELICS
Perhaps the only object known for certain to have come from the vessel itself is the 4pdr gun on view at Greenwich. This was one of six guns thrown overboard to lighten the ship when she ran aground on the Endeavour Reef on 11 June 1770. In 1969, 199 years afterwards, these six guns were brought to the surface by a team of American divers. One of these guns was presented to the National Maritime Museum, where it may be seen and measured.

MODELS
To commemorate the charting of New Zealand by Cook, the National Maritime Museum presented a 1/24 scale model to that country in 1969.

Below: The *Endeavour* drawn up for repairs after grounding on the Australian coast.

By courtesy of Cassel Caravel and The British Museum

Three views showing the high quality of workmanship and the wealth of detail incorporated and, below, the cutaway model showing the internal arrangements.

All photos by courtesy of the author.

Mr C W Whiticker built a 1/48 scale model of the *Endeavour* during the 1930s and for some time this was on view at Australia House in London; its present whereabouts are uncertain. During the 1975 NMM Model Competition Mr S Hodgeson was highly commended for his entry of an *Endeavour* which although unfinished at the time, showed great promise for a 16-year-old modeller.

In 1973 the author was commissioned by the National Maritime Museum to build a model of the *Endeavour*. This model was completed in 1976 and is now housed in the museum. It took 3100 hours to build and is displayed to show the starboard side open to reveal the lower decks and hold with representative stores and ballast in position. The port side represents the finished ship set in a sea with long boat alongside.

WARSHIP FITTINGS

by Don Brown

Don Brown's destroyer models are frequent winners at rallies and exhibitions, where the quality of his detail-work is often remarked upon. This short description of how he makes some of his small fittings is a 'pilot study' for his chapter on 'Deck Fittings' in the forthcoming book 'Scale Model Warships'.

In this article I propose to describe my methods of modelling anchors and associated equipment for nineteenth and twentieth century warships. The intention is to illustrate my approach to the problems presented: how I break down a complex shape as far as possible into a number of pieces, each reasonably simple to produce. The methods are equally applicable to such fittings in all types of vessels.

Firstly, a note in measuring fittings from drawings and photographs. I believe the traditional way of lifting a dimension is with a pair of dividers; this may be admirable for hull and superstructure dimensions but not so for fittings. Despite ridicule from some quarters about unneccessary accuracy, in my experience the most useful tool for this purpose is a micrometer. It does not need much practice to split the lines when measuring from a drawing and, having done so, it is certainly the most convenient tool for checking your workpiece. It is also useful, when making components indicated on the drawing by a single line, to remember that when working to a scale of 1/8 in = 1 ft, for all practical purposes ten thousandths of an inch represents one inch full size, and that a 3 in scupper pipe, for instance, would be well represented by a 30 thou wire.

Before dealing with actual fittings, a word about materials. I am a firm believer in building light and ballasting a model down to her marks; this way a stable model is produced that looks right on the water. How often does one see a

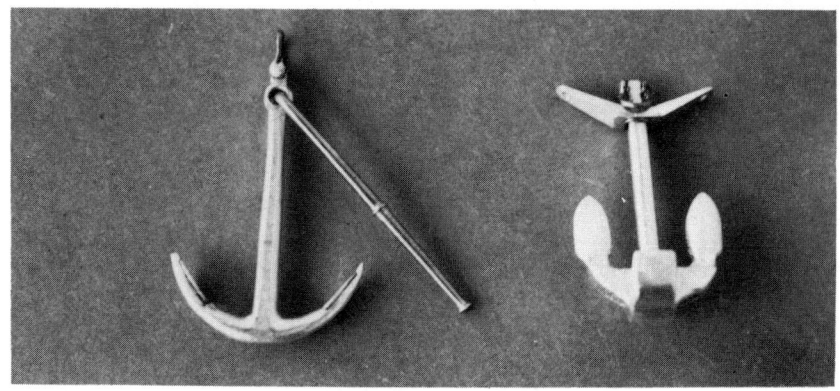

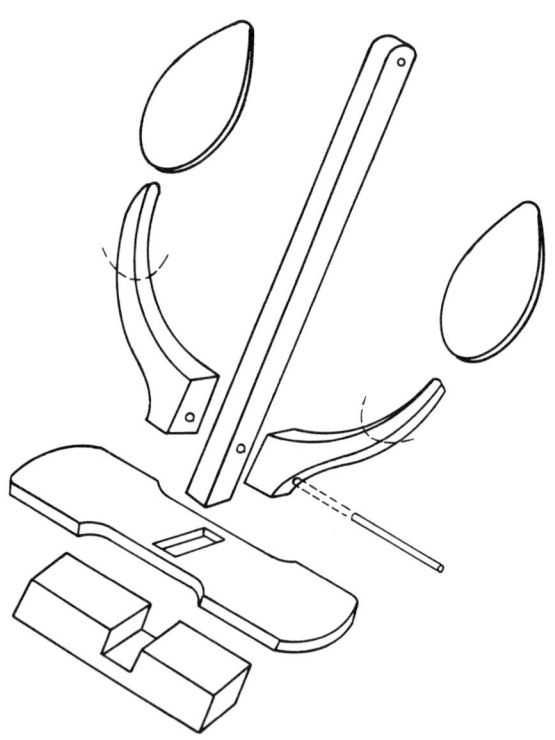

HALL'S STOCKLESS ANCHOR

nice model that is tender on the water and heels alarmingly in the slightest cross wind, usually the result of heavy superstructure and brass fittings. I favour the use of aluminium for sheet work and aluminium alloy for turned or filed work. It is light, much lighter than plastic, crisp and nice to work and can be satisfactorily joined with an epoxy resin adhesive (preferably not the rapid hardening variety).

ANCHORS

The majority of anchors in use are of the flat stowing type and I will use as an example the Hall's stockless anchor. To avoid a too complex filing operation a start should be made by cutting and filing the arms to shape from a piece of metal of suitable thickness. This should include the outer ends of the arms which form the ribs to the flukes. I find it best to make the two arms together out of one piece, cutting through the centre after drilling for the hinge pin. The arms are first filed up with a rectangular section until the desired shape is obtained and then rounded off and finally slotted at the ends with a piercing saw to receive the flukes.

The shaft is a straightforward component cut from thick sheet metal filed to shape in sections if necessary and drilled for hinge pin and shackle. The tripping plate is made from a separate piece of sheet metal filed to profile with a rectangular perforation drilled and filed in the centre to pass the end of the shaft. Similarly, a separate rectangular section 'weight' is cut, slotted for the end of the shaft and fixed to the underside of the tripping plate.

Finally, flukes are cut and filed from thin sheet metal and a shackle bent up from wire.

CAPSTANS

When making a capstan I find it best to work from a series of washers and bosses of various thicknesses and mount the whole on a short length of studding for fixing to the deck. Indeed in this manner the capstan may be used for fixing removable decks in position or for operating a switch. The washers can either be bent from sheet metal of suitable

thickness, finished off by mounting on a mandrel in either a drill or lathe, or alternatively sliced off in the lathe from a drilled rod.

Tops of capstans vary and in the sketch the top washer indicates one of many. If it is desired to add the bolts to the upper surface of the top plate this can be done by drilling a series of holes around the perimeter, fixing short lengths of wire in the holes with epoxy resin, and filing off to length after the adhesive has hardened. If the holes are countersunk on the underside it leaves room for a little more adhesive and produces a firmer joint; indeed I have found this method satisfactory for 'bolts' down to 15 thou diameter.

The second washer has notches filed in the edge and when sandwiched between the top and a plain washer produces the square holes required for the capstan bars.

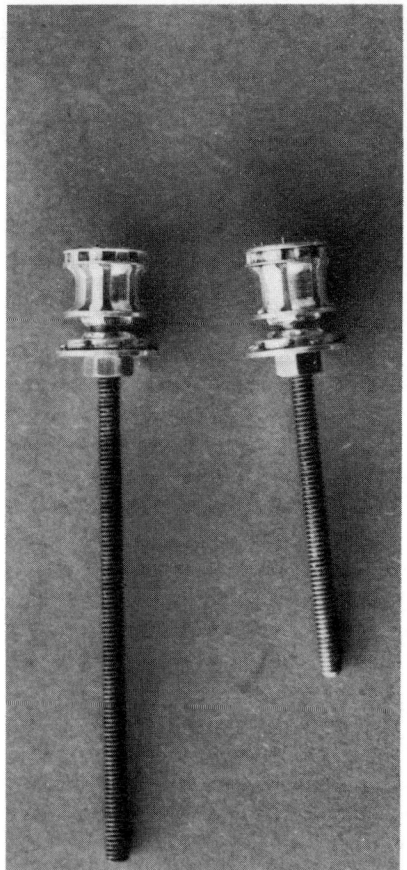

Opposite and right: Anchors and capstans

CAPSTAN		DIA. MM	THK	DIA. "THOU"	THK
SHAPED TOP WASHER		9·4	0·5	370	20
WASHER NOTCHED FOR CAPSTAN BARS		8·9	1·0	350	40
PLAIN WASHER		9·4	0·25	370	10
SLOTTED WARPING DRUM		7·0 to 8·9	5·0	280 to 350	200
PLAIN WASHER		9·4	0·5	370	20
"STAR" GYPSY WASHER ⌀		6·6	0·75	260	30
SPACER		3·2	0·75	125	30
"STAR" GYPSY WASHER ⌀		6·6	0·75	260	30
PLAIN WASHER DRILLED AND FITTED WITH WIRE PAWLS		9·4	1·0	370	40
PLAIN WASHER FIXED TO DECK		11·3	0·5	445	20

⌀ NOTE: CORNERS OF "TEETH" TO BE SLIGHTLY ROUNDED

The warping drum is made in a similar manner. A shaped boss is turned, drilled through the centre and finally saw cuts are made vertically to represent the segments bolted on in the prototype. In some older types of capstan the drum appears to be a casting with a series of vertical ridges. This is made in exactly the same manner and small pieces of sheet metal are epoxied into the slots and filed to profile just proud of the drum.

The chain gypsy is built up from two washers with a spacer between. The washers are first filed into hexagons and then the flats are filed concave with a half round needle file; finally the corners of the 'teeth' are slightly rounded on the edge facing the spacer.

The moving part of the capstan is completed with a fairly thick washer which may be drilled around the perimeter to receive tiny pieces of bent wire to represent pawls. The sketch illustrates the various components described and gives suitably proportioned sizes for a fairly large capstan as used in some nineteenth century cruisers to a scale of 1/8 in = 1 ft.

HAWSE PIPES

A reasonable scale representation of hawse pipes tends to be neglected. Usually a metal tube, sometimes squashed oval, is inserted through holes in deck and hull and cut off flush. However this rarely produces the true shape. I have used two methods.

Method 1 Used where deck and side plating holes are not too close together. After cutting the proper shaped holes in both deck and hull plating, cut a small block of wood with splayed ends so that it fits nicely in the angle between deck and hull with the grain in the direction of the pipe. Hold in position and draw the shape of the two holes in the ends of the block. Remove the block and carve a female mould using the end outlines as guides; the result will look something like a leg of lamb. After sanding the mould coat it liberally with wax and then cover with cataloy paste. When the paste has set, file both ends to the angle of and to expose the ends of the mould and remove the mould. This is achieved by making two longitudinal cuts with a piercing saw, carefully prizing off the half hawse pipes and glueing the two halves back together with cataloy paste. The completed pipes can be glued in position with more paste and finally trimmed to the lines of the deck and hull holes with an abrafile.

Method 2 Used where the deck and side holes are close together. Again cut the proper shaped holes in both deck and hull plating and form a rough box with balsa wood connecting the two holes. Liberally line this box with cataloy paste applied through the holes and after the paste has set file to a neat pipe with an abrafile.

In both cases the holes through hull and deck should be finished with a half round bead. This is made from a length of suitable gauge copper wire held in a piercing saw in place of the blade and filed to half section supported on a block of wood.

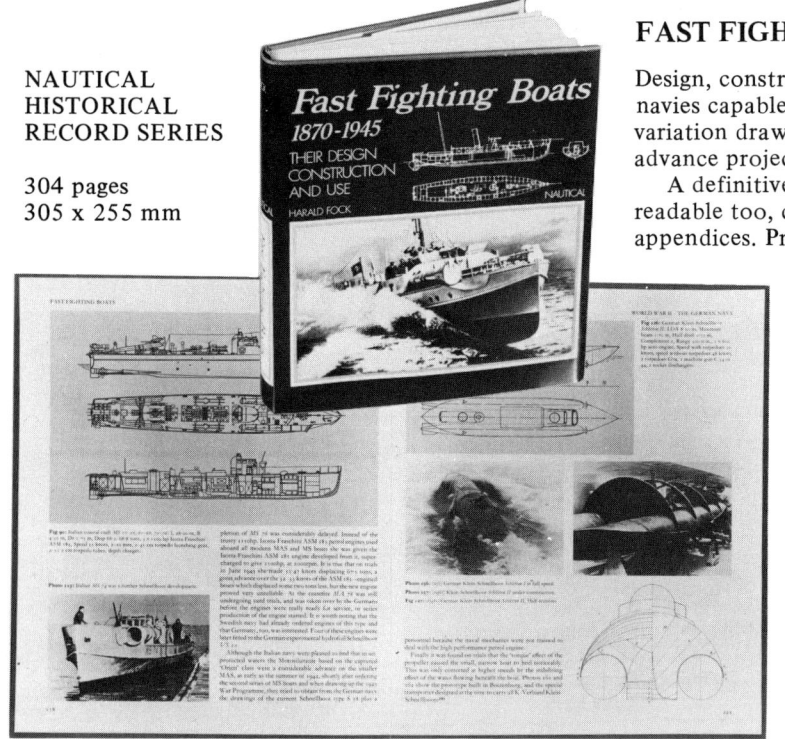

HMS CROCODILE, 24 (1781)

by Keith Hobbs

Although the sea has been his profession, Keith Hobbs (Master mariner) is keenly interested in the shipbuilding techniques of the 18th century, and in building models of vessels of this period.

Continuing my notes about some of the various fittings which I have made for my model of HMS *Crocodile,* I shall deal this time with the rough tree rail and the capstans.

The Capstan

These, I discovered upon close examination of the draught (Admiralty Draught 2868, Box 43, scale ¼ in = 1 ft), differed from each other. The main deck capstan had six whelps whereas the one directly above and connected to it on the quarterdeck, had only four. Also the drum-head of the latter was a greater diameter than the trundle-head of the lower one. The mortices for the bars do not coincide with each capstan but are rotated 30 degrees from each other and their axis was not vertical but perpendicular to the sheer-line.

In spite of the well-executed and detailed drawing noteworthy in this draught, I could see no indication of pawls or a pawl-plate. Falconer shows pawls which can be pushed in against the whelps for a similar type of capstan. Primarily, the function of the capstan was weighing anchor, but it also carried out a variety of other work. As I see it, its position was governed by three main factors:
1. The necessity to be on the same deck as the hawse holes.
2. The need for sufficient 'drift' for the messenger to be nipped to the cable.
3. A clear area to give working space for the sweep of the capstan bars.

A second ancillary capstan was also desirable in working the ship and the siting of this above the other and connected to it was very practical. Not only did it give added support to the main capstan below but it was possible to duplicate the manning; in addition to the six bars of the lower capstan, six more on the upper one could also be manned, giving considerable power when needed. Four men to each bar would mean a total of 48 men to weigh the 29½ cwt bower anchor. The positioning of the bars in relation to the two capstans would assist in more even power applied by the men, particularly when the vessel was riding to a rough sea.

Because the heavy hemp cable was so large — 15 in circumference for a Sixth Rate — it was not possible to take turns of it directly on the whelps so a 'messenger' — a cable-laid rope about 8 in circumference in this case — was employed. (Chain cable did not come into use in the Royal Navy until 1811.) This took the form of an endless whip having four turns around the capstan and then led right forward ahead of the manger and around leads just abaft the hawse holes. (Rollers were introduced in 1792†.) The manger was a small space confined by a low bulkhead a short distance abaft the hawse-holes to prevent water sweeping aft along the deck as the ship dipped into a sea. Large scuppers either side allowed water to escape

† A R Bugler in his book on the restoration of the *Victory.*

freely. This space was also used to wash off the mud and weed from the cable as it 'came home'. The cable was stopped to the messenger by short braided ropes called 'nippers' held by boys who, depending on the weight on the cable, walked or ran along the deck with it as it 'came home'. As their part of the cable reached the main hatch where it was fed down and stowed in the hold on dunnage to assist drying, the boys whipped off their stoppers and smartly returned 'forrard' to nip another bight of cable.

Capstan bars were slotted at their outer ends to take rope called a 'swifter' which was bound around them to prevent their coming out when working. (Alan Villiers in *Sons of Sinbad* mentions a capstan aboard a 'boom' taking charge and the capstan bars flying in all directions. Presumably the Arabs did not use swifters!)

As well as anchor work, this essential piece of equipment was doubtless used for such heavy work as taking out and stepping the lower masts when dockyard facilities were not available, warping and springing ship, and hoisting boats. Whether it was thought, as in the case of this ship, that four instead of six whelps were all that were necessary, as the workload of the quarterdeck capstan was not as heavy, I don't know. It may have been standard practice in these smaller rates. The type of work carried out by this upper capstan would have been the setting up of yards, 'hardening up' the jeers, sending up topmasts, hauling on braces, loading stores, raising guns from the hold and so on.

THE CONSTRUCTION

As with most aspects in model building I find there are few short cuts and, in the long run, it is often quicker and certainly more satisfying to construct or build up most items even if at first glance they might be considered of no great consequence. In line with my usual practice I began by making working drawings.

If the item is to be left unpainted I try to use different woods for the various parts, for I think doing so adds interest. In this instance I used a scrap of boxwood for the barrel, blackwood for the whelps, mahogany for the drum and trundle heads, and ebony for the cap. The barrel I rebated to take the whelps as shown

in the drawing. To space them evenly I used a piece of paper equal in length to the circumference of the barrel and marked out for four or six spaces as required. The square mortice holes for the bars in the heads were each made with separate pieces of wood centred and glued on thin solid pieces top and bottom, and then turned to size on a lathe.

I made a jig for the whelps from a scrap of hacksaw blade and cut tenons in them to fit the rebates on the barrel. Separate pieces were used in the partners and laid athwartships The strengthening pieces between the whelps were cut with 60 or 90 degree angles, the outer rim cut roughly to shape and trimmed after assembly. The whole job gave me a lot of pleasure.

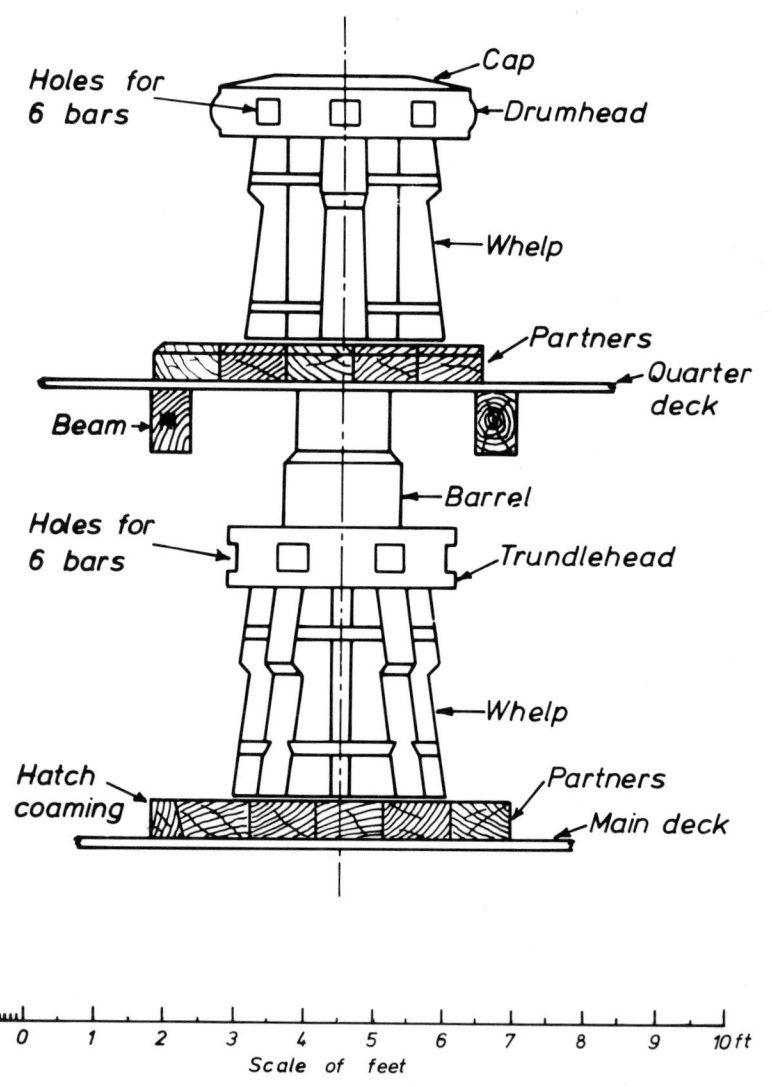

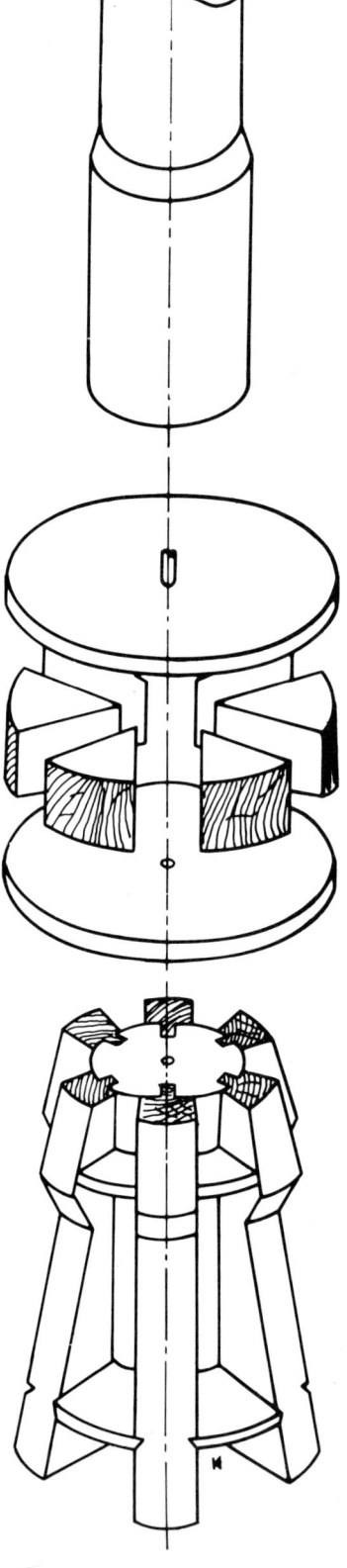

Scale of feet

The Rough Tree Rail

It will be seen that the rail diminishes in height above the plank sheer towards the stern and calls for stanchions of varying lengths (Figure 1). At the fore end it finishes in a graceful curve to the plank sheer. I wished to make it all from ebony, which is brittle but polishes well and is an excellent way to highlight features in a dockyard model.

Like most tasks the job became much simpler when I thought of a method of tackling it. First I began with the stanchions by shaping pieces of ebony as shown in Figure 2 and cutting off in a jig along the dotted lines and numbering them to correspond with the plan. Distance 'a¹' corresponds with 'a' in Figure 1 as do 'b¹' and 'b'. I allowed a little extra in length. Their side elevation then appeared as in Figure 4.

In order to get the correct height for each stanchion and to trim the tops and bottoms correctly for each position, (eg those at the gun position have one side vertical), I made a jig from hardwood conforming to the area enclosed between the top of the plank sheer and the underside of the rough tree rail, Figure 5. The cut out sections were done carefully to ensure a tight fit for the stanchions.

Next, the stanchions were placed in the jig (Figure 6) and trimmed to size with abrasive paper glued to a strip of wood. The rail itself was cut to a little oversize and trimmed down evenly with the aid of the scrapers (Figure 7). To ensure the whole assembly would be strong and rigid I used copper dowels, top and bottom, with Araldite as the adhesive. The shaped fore ends of the rails were carved and lap jointed at the stanchions and dowelled to the plank sheer.

With the work involved one might well ponder on the term 'rough tree rail'. It may have been such in ships of a much earlier era but could it be that this adherence of an old term is another example of the conservativeness of seafarers?

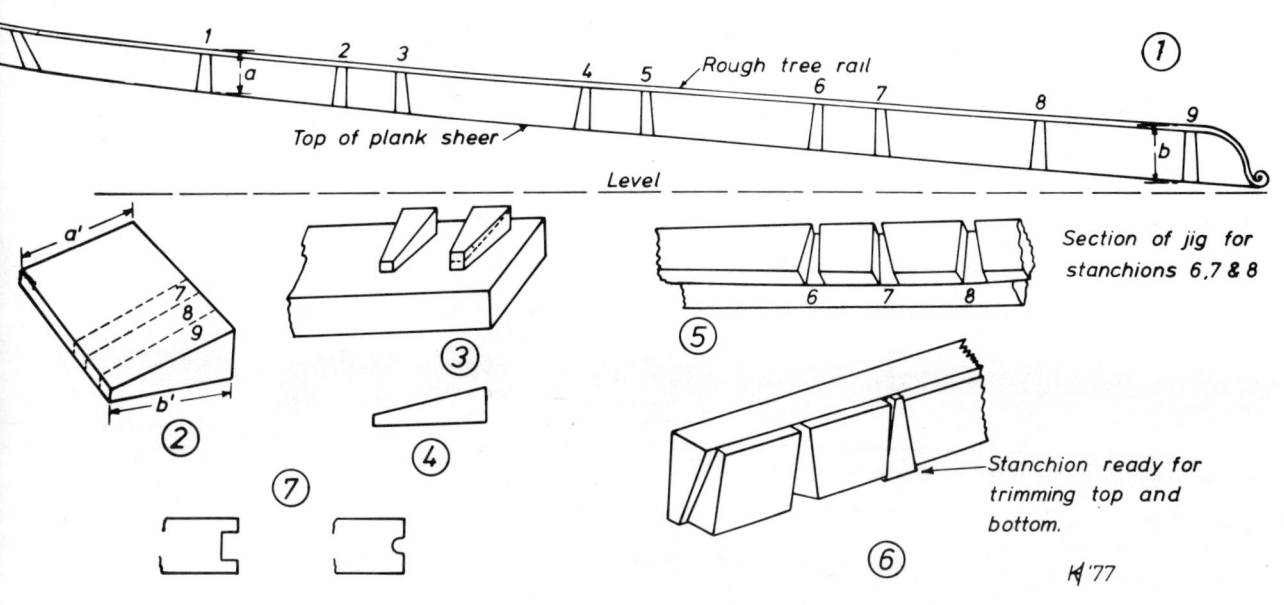

Rough tree rail

Top of plank sheer

Level

Section of jig for stanchions 6,7 & 8

Stanchion ready for trimming top and bottom.

H '77

SHIP MODELERS ASSOCIATES

38 HARTFORD AVENUE
WETHERSFIELD, CONN. 06109
USA

The Widest Selection of Plans Available in the USA ~ Now from SMA

Ship Modelers Associates has rapidly become the LARGEST company in the UNITED STATES which is solely devoted to providing only the materials required by the MODEL SHIP BUILDER. Our PLAN department is the most complete in the world, offering drawings by such notables as, **MacGregor, Lusci, Underhill, Gay, Channing, Leavitt, Musees de la Marine, Mantua/Sergal, Corel, Art Amb Fusta, Rielly, Breisinger, Campbell,** and we will soon be offering a completely new line of drawings, never before shown, for the builder of R/C model. These will be 1/2'' = 1' sc.

SMA is also proud to hold **EXCLUSIVE North American sales** rights for the extremely fine modeling plans by **Dr. Alvaro Matteucci (A-MODEL).**

Many of these plans are suitable for both static and navigable building.

We have complete access to plans by **Mr. F. Less'Ard,** again among the most detailed and informative renderings available; the highly detailed plans by **Mr. Wm.L. Crothers (Sea-Gull)** may be purchased through SMA.

In order to be the only FULL SERVICE firm for the ship modeler, we also offer a complete line of books, tools, rigging and fittings, kits from the U.S. and plank-on-frame from abroad, woods, and all of the advice that out experienced staff willingly offers.

A CATALOG (NEWSLETTER), which is never complete, is offered for a one time charge of S6.00 postpaid. This catalog now has two folders, the first of approx. 115 pages and our second, being printed, approx. 27 pages with many more to follow: automatically mailed to you at no additional cost, periodically as new items of interest become available.

OUR SALES POLICY is SERVICE and COMPLETE CUSTOMER SATISFACTION or your money is refunded if our products do not meet your standards or arrive damaged. This policy is extended throughout the world.

All orders must be paid for by INTERNATIONAL MONEY ORDERS or CHECKS payable to 'SMA' in U.S. dollars, ONLY. Since all correspondence is personally answered, please allow occasional delays, but we do respond.

For total SERVICE and SATISFACTION, you do not have to look further than **'SMA'.**

NEW BOOKS

CONWAY MARITIME

New Sailing Ship and Modelmaking Titles
The following three books are acknowledged by modelmakers and enthusiasts to be classics in their field, and originals are now expensive collectors' items. They contain unique and detailed information and are illustrated in depth with plans, drawings and photographs. These large format reprints are designed to preserve the clarity and detail of the original illustrations and to make them available once more at a reasonable price.

SHIPS OF THE PAST by Charles G Davis
A study in a degree of detail to satisfy the most exacting modelmaker - of a range of local sailing craft, schooner, packet ships and naval frigates. Appendix on sources for plans.
10¾" × 8¼", 188 pages, 43 photos, 33 plans and 55 line drawings.
Available March £5.50 (plus 50p post and packing)

THE FRIGATE CONSTITUTION and other Historic Ships by F Alexander Magoun
An anatomy of the construction of the oldest warship still afloat, by the man who drew up the plans for her reconstruction. A full set of plans are included, and the book also covers a Viking longship, *Santa Maria, Mayflower,* the clipper *Flying Cloud* and the schooner *Bluenose*
10¾" × 8¼", 156 pages, 30 photos, 16 plans and 63 line drawings.
Available March £5.50 (plus 50p postage and packing)

THE BALTIMORE CLIPPER by Howard Chappelle
The definitive study of the privateering, smuggling, slaving and blockade-running schooners that were built first and foremost for speed. Many detailed plans by the author, who was probably the most eminent authority on sailing craft in the world.
10¾" × 8¼", 200 pages, 36 photos and 48 plans. **Available March** £5.50 (plus 50p post and packing)

MODEL SHIPWRIGHT 23 edited by John Bowen.
The latest edition of the only quarterly devoted to scale ship modelling of the highest quality.
Available March £2.25 (including postage) or only £7 for a full annual subscription. (In North America, available from S.M.A., 38 Hartford Avenue, Wethersfield, Connecticut 06109, at $4.50 or $18.00 respectively.)

SAILING SHIPS ON OLD POSTCARDS [**Segelschiffe auf alten postkarten**] by Jürgen Meyer
A magnificent collection of 610 postcards, depicting European sailing ships of the 19th and 20th centuries. Issued in this country for the first time, it is an unusual and delightful reference - a genuine collector's item.
10½" × 12", 200 pages. **Available March** £25.00 [**plus £1.00 post and packing**]

Please add the post and packing if ordering direct from:
Dept. MS
CONWAY MARITIME PRESS LTD.
2 NELSON ROAD
GREENWICH
London SE10 9JB
UK
(Tel: 01-858 7211)